Houghton Mifflin

*Montel*

# EXPLORE

## LITERACY ACTIVITY BOOK

**Senior Authors**
J. David Cooper
John J. Pikulski

**Authors**
Kathryn H. Au
Margarita Calderón
Jacqueline C. Comas
Marjorie Y. Lipson
J. Sabrina Mims
Susan E. Page
Sheila W. Valencia
MaryEllen Vogt

**Consultants**
Dolores Malcolm
Tina Saldivar
Shane Templeton

INVITATIONS TO LITERACY

**Houghton Mifflin Company • Boston**

Atlanta  •  Dallas  •  Geneva, Illinois  •  Palo Alto  •  Princeton

*Illustration Credits*

Leo Abbett 247, 250; Susan Aiello Theme Icons, 7, 56, 83, 84, 131; Andrea Barrett 179; Shirley Beckes 236, 240, 242; Karen Bell/Carolyn Potts & Associates 13; Paulette Bogan 211, 227; Chuck Brache/Steven Edsey & Sons 216; Cindy Brodie/Square Moon Productions 131; Ruth Brunke 19, 25, 28, 105, 121, 127, 152, 156, 157, 173, 174, 186, 223, 237, 241, 243, 246, 252; Robert Burger/Deborah Wolfe 12, 15, 112, 124, 219; Jannine Cabossel 100; Tony Caldwell/Cornell & McCarthy 181; Olivia Cole/Asciutto Art Reps 137, 199; Daniel Collins 188, 189, 192; Mike Dammer/Steven Edsey & Sons 198, 202; Ruta Daugavietis 63, 132. 149, 153, 230, 231; Shelly Dieterichs-Morrison 39; Tom Duckworth 54, 69, 72, 79, 85, 95, 108, 114, 122, 141, 166, 207, 251, 253, 256; George Eisner/Steven Edsey & Sons 73, 76, 95; Kate Flanagan/Cornell & McCarthy 192, 194, 195; Bryan Friel/Steven Edsey & Sons 101; Dave Garbot iv, 2, 203, 224; Steve Gillig 235; Susan Greenstein 144, 146; Gary Hamilton 104, 175, 177, 193, 196; Paul Hoffman 123; Robin Hotchkiss/Deborah Wolfe 232; Bob Lange 32, 38, 40, 59, 63, 96, 162, 169, 227, 228; Jared D. Lee 103; Bert Mayse iv, 49, 51, 110, 139, 178, 183, 190, 204, 234; Lori Mitchell 45, 50, 53; Paul Moch 4, 34, 36, 55, 64, 130, 150; Andy Myer/Deborah Wolfe 213, 215, 218; Carol O'Malia 233, 239; Hank Parker/Steven Edsey & Sons191, 196, 197; Mike Quon 232; Stephen Schudlich/Ceci Bartels Associates 135, 136, 160; Jack Scott 96; Neil Shigley/Carol Chislovsky 151, 155; Scott Snow/Creative Freelancers 19, 86, 93; Mike Sobey/Steven Edsey & Sons 168, 217, 221; Darren Thompson iii, 3, 5, 43, 44, 71, 75, 201, 205; George Thompson 87, 147, 238; George Ulrich/HK Portfolio 17, 18, 46, 97, 111, 116, 137, 180; Quentin Webb/Creative Freelancers iii, 61, 62, 100, 226, 229; Dave Winter 23, 52, 77, 91, 109, 194, 220, 222, 254.

*Photo Credits*

©Alfred M. Bailey from National Audubon Society/Photo Researchers, Inc., 17; ©BPS Ltd./H. Armstrong Roberts, Inc., 143; ©Allan D. Cruickshank from National Audobon Society/Photo Researchers, Inc., 202; ©Tomas del Amo/H. Armstrong Roberts, Inc., iii, top left, 20; ©Tony Freeman/PhotoEdit, 203, top right; ©Francois Gohier/Photo Researchers, Inc., 206; ©A. Gurmankin/Unicorn Stock Photos, 114; ©H. Armstrong Roberts, Inc., 221, inset; ©Hella Hammio/Photo Researchers, Inc., 167; ©Ed Harp/Unicorn Stock Photos, 47, top left; ©Hoeoeck/Mauritius/H. Armstrong Roberts, Inc., 208, top; ©Image Club Graphics, Inc., 141, 230; ©Gary Irving/Tony Stone Images, 129; ©1971 Karl H. Maslowski/Photo Researchers, Inc., 16; ©Tom McHugh/Photo Researchers, Inc., 151; ©Will & Deni McIntyre/Photo Researchers, Inc., 155; ©NASA, 33, top left, 164, 166, 171; ©NASA/Jupiter Productions, 33, all other, 35; ©Michael Newman/PhotoEdit, 140; ©Courtesy of the George C. Page Museum/Natural History Museum of Los Angeles County, 247, 248; ©PhotoDisc, 60, 76, 88, 92, 97, top, 102, 118, right, 126; ©Rod Planck/Tony Stone Images, 107; ©Maresa Pryor/Animals/Animals, 47, bottom right; ©Leonard Lee RueIII from National Audobon Society/Photo Researchers, Inc., 56; ©M. Schneiders/H. Armstrong Roberts, Inc., iv, 184; ©Jim Stamates/Tony Stone Images, 50; ©1986 Norm Thomas/Photo Researchers, Inc., 14; ©Rob Tringali Jr./Sports Chrome Inc., 119, top; ©David Young-Wolff/PhotoEdit, 144; All other photographs by Ralph J. Brunke.

1997 Impression

Copyright © 1996 by Houghton Mifflin Company. All rights reserved.

Printed in the U.S.A.

ISBN: 0-395-72486-4

56789-WC-99 98 97 96

# CONTENTS

**Introductory Selection    A Package for Mrs. Jewls**

Reading Strategy Guide . . . . . . . . . . . . . . . . . . . . . . 1

Selection Vocabulary . . . . . . . . . . . . . . . . . . . . . . . 2

Comprehension Check . . . . . . . . . . . . . . . . . . . . . . 3

Reading-Writing Workshop: A Class Book

The Writing Process . . . . . . . . . . . . . . . . . . . . . . . 4

Prewriting . . . . . . . . . . . . . . . . . . . . . . . . . . . . . . 5

Revising . . . . . . . . . . . . . . . . . . . . . . . . . . . . . . . 6

**Theme 1    Journey to Adventure!**

Selection Connections . . . . . . . . . . . . . . . . . . . . . 7

**James and the Giant Peach** . . . . . . . . . . . . . . . . 9

**Arctic Explorer: The Story of Matthew Henson** . . . . . 19

Reading-Writing Workshop: A Personal Essay . . . . . . 29

**Voyager: An Adventure to the Edge of the**

**Solar System** . . . . . . . . . . . . . . . . . . . . . . . . . 32

Theme Wrap-Up . . . . . . . . . . . . . . . . . . . . . . . . . 42

**Theme 2    In the Wild**

Selection Connections . . . . . . . . . . . . . . . . . . . . . 43

**Wolves** . . . . . . . . . . . . . . . . . . . . . . . . . . . . . . . 45

**The Midnight Fox** . . . . . . . . . . . . . . . . . . . . . . . 55

Reading-Writing Workshop: Persuasion . . . . . . . . . . 65

**Adiós falcón/Good-bye, Falcon** . . . . . . . . . . . . . . 69

Theme Wrap-Up . . . . . . . . . . . . . . . . . . . . . . . . . 81

**Theme 3    Try to See It My Way**

Selection Connections . . . . . . . . . . . . . . . . . . . . . 83

**In the Year of the Boar and Jackie Robinson** . . . . . . 85

Reading-Writing Workshop: A Description . . . . . . . . 97

**Like Jake and Me** . . . . . . . . . . . . . . . . . . . . . . . 100

**Me, Mop, and the Moondance Kid** . . . . . . . . . . . . 111

**Felita** . . . . . . . . . . . . . . . . . . . . . . . . . . . . . . . 121

Theme Wrap-Up . . . . . . . . . . . . . . . . . . . . . . . . . 133

# CONTENTS

**Theme 4  Catastrophe!**

Selection Connections . . . . . . . . . . . . . . . . . . . . . . . . 135
**Night of the Twisters** . . . . . . . . . . . . . . . . . . . . . 137
**Earthquakes** . . . . . . . . . . . . . . . . . . . . . . . . . 148
Reading-Writing Workshop: A Research Report . . . . 159
**The Story of the *Challenger* Disaster** . . . . . . . . . . 162
Theme Wrap-Up . . . . . . . . . . . . . . . . . . . . . . . . . 172

**Theme 5  From the Prairie to the Sea**

Selection Connections . . . . . . . . . . . . . . . . . . . . . . . . 173
**Along the Santa Fe Trail** . . . . . . . . . . . . . . . . . . 175
Reading-Writing Workshop: A Personal Narrative . . 185
**Children of the Wild West** . . . . . . . . . . . . . . . . . 188
**Pecos Bill** . . . . . . . . . . . . . . . . . . . . . . . . . . . . 198
Theme Wrap-Up . . . . . . . . . . . . . . . . . . . . . . . . . 209

**Theme 6  Do You *Believe* This??**

Selection Connections . . . . . . . . . . . . . . . . . . . . . . . . 211
**La Bamba** . . . . . . . . . . . . . . . . . . . . . . . . . . . . 213
**Willie Bea and the Time the Martians Landed** . . . . . 223
**McBroom Tells the Truth** . . . . . . . . . . . . . . . . . . 233
Reading-Writing Workshop: A Story . . . . . . . . . . . . 243
**Trapped in Tar: Fossils of the Ice Age** . . . . . . . . . . 246
Theme Wrap-Up . . . . . . . . . . . . . . . . . . . . . . . . . 256

**Student Handbook** . . . . . . . . . . . . . . . . . . . . . . . . . . 257
Independent Reading Log . . . . . . . . . . . . . . . . . . . . 259
Spelling Guide . . . . . . . . . . . . . . . . . . . . . . . . . . . 263
Grammar Guide . . . . . . . . . . . . . . . . . . . . . . . . . . 284
    A Resource for Grammar, Usage,
    Capitalization, and Punctuation
Proofreading Checklist . . . . . . . . . . . . . . . . . . . . . 316
Proofreading Marks . . . . . . . . . . . . . . . . . . . . . . . 316

Name

# My Reading Strategy Guide

✔ As I **Predict/Infer**, I . . .
- ❑ Look for important information.
- ❑ Look at illustrations.
- ❑ Think about what I know.
- ❑ Think about what will happen next.

✔ As I read, I **Self-Question** and . . .
- ❑ Ask questions to answer for myself as I go along.

✔ As I read and **Think About Words**, I . . .
- ❑ Figure out words by using context, sounds, and word parts.
- ❑ Think of similar words.
- ❑ Read to the end of the sentence or paragraph.
- ❑ Look at the illustrations.

✔ As I **Monitor** my reading, I ask . . .
- ❑ Does this make sense to me?
- ❑ Does it help me meet my purpose?

I try fix-ups:
- ❑ Reread.
- ❑ Read ahead.
- ❑ Look at illustrations.
- ❑ Ask for help.

✔ During and after reading, I **Summarize** and . . .
- ❑ For stories, I think about story elements.
- ❑ For informational texts, I think about main ideas and important details.

✔ As I read, I **Evaluate** and ask myself . . .
- ❑ How do I feel about what I read?
- ❑ Do I agree or disagree with it?
- ❑ How does this compare with similar types of writing that I've read?

Name

# Are You Gasping for Words?

Use a vocabulary word to write a sentence that tells what is happening in each picture.

faint      wobbled
numb      staggered
huffed    collapsed

**1** _____
_____

**4** _____
_____

**2** _____
_____

**5** _____
_____

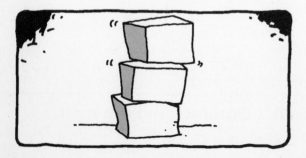

**3** _____
_____

**6** _____
_____

.................................................................
Name

# Wayside School Days

Answer the questions about "A Package for Mrs. Jewls."

What was Louis doing when the truck drove up?

_____

_____

_____

What happened to Louis on the fifteenth floor?

_____

_____

_____

Why wasn't Miss Zarves in her classroom?

_____

_____

_____

Why did Louis have to wait such a long time for
someone to open the door to Mrs. Jewls's classroom?

_____

_____

_____

Draw a picture and write a
sentence that tell what happens
at the end of the story.

_____

_____

_____

Name

# The Writing Process

**Prewriting**
Choose a topic and plan your writing.

**Drafting**
Now you can write! Get your ideas down quickly. Don't worry if you make errors. Have fun! Be creative!

**Revising**
Read your draft. How can you make your ideas clearer? Should you move anything to improve the order? Can you use stronger words? Should you add or remove anything?

**Proofreading**
Read your draft carefully. Look for spelling, grammar, and punctuation errors. Correct these using proofreading marks. You may want to proofread twice.

**Publishing and Sharing**
Give your piece a good title and make a final copy. Have fun publishing it! Share it and display it.

Name

# Get Started!

**Choose a Topic**  List three or four choices you might like to write about.

**1** _____    **3** _____

**2** _____    **4** _____

**Plan Your Writing**  Write your topic on the box top.  Then write a few sentences about the beginning, the middle, and the end of the incident in each panel.

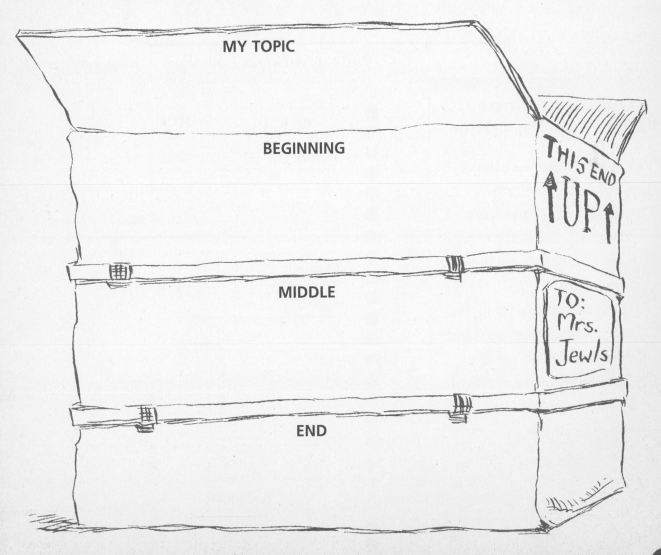

MY TOPIC

BEGINNING

MIDDLE

END

THIS END
↑UP↑

TO: Mrs. Jewls

Name

# Revising Your Writing

Reread and revise your story. Use the Revising Checklist as a guide.
Then have a writing conference with a classmate. Use the
Questions for a Writing Conference to guide the discussion.

## Revising Checklist

☐ Is the writing easy to understand?

☐ Should I leave anything out?

☐ Do I need to add anything?

☐ Does the writing have a beginning, a middle, and an end?

☐ Do I need to replace uninteresting words?

**Write down ideas from your writing conference.**

## Questions for a Writing Conference

- What is the best thing about this writing?
- What makes the story funny?
- How well is the writing organized?
- Are all the events in the story easy to understand?
- How effective are the beginning, the middle, and the end?
- What suggestions might improve the writing?

## Notes

_____

_____

_____

_____

_____

_____

_____

_____

_____

_____

Name

# Journey to Adventure!

After reading each selection, complete the chart below and on the next page to show what you discovered.

| | What qualities do the adventurers in the selection have? | Where does the adventure take place? |
|---|---|---|
| James and the Giant Peach | | |
| Arctic Explorer: The Story of Matthew Henson | | |
| Voyager: An Adventure to the Edge of the Solar System | | |

Name

# Journey to Adventure!

After reading each selection, complete the chart to show what
you discovered.

| | What risks or challenges do the adventurers in the selection face? | How do the adventurers overcome dangers and complete their adventure? |
|---|---|---|
| **James and the Giant Peach** | | |
| **Arctic Explorer: The Story of Matthew Henson** | | |
| **Voyager: An Adventure to the Edge of the Solar System** | | |

What have you learned in this theme about facing challenges and
overcoming obstacles?

_____

_____

_____

# Dangerous Words

Use words from the box to complete the sentences and
send the characters on a journey to adventure!  At the end
of each paragraph, add a sentence to the story.

pandemonium
exhorting
lunge
tethered
aghast

A storm was approaching.  Pete and Gale had just _____ their

boat to the dock when a giant wave hit.  Suddenly the rope they had used to tie the boat to the

dock snapped! _____

_____

Pete and Gale made a _____ for the dock, but it was just out of

reach. They began to drift out to sea. _____

_____

They rowed their boat as fast as they could, _____ each

other to row faster.  However, the wind and waves were too strong. _____

_____

Sharks began to circle the boat.  Pete and Gale were _____,

shocked by what was happening. _____

_____

The waves began to crash over the boat.  Panic and _____

broke out. Just as they were about to give up hope, Gale had an idea. _____

_____

**Describe a situation that would make you frantic.**

_____

_____

_____

Name

# Capture the Captions

These illustrations show some of the events in *James and the Giant Peach.*  Write captions that describe the illustrations.

# Flying Peaches

James wanted to make a peach fly. The steps of his plan have been provided. Show the proper sequence by numbering them. The first step has been numbered for you.

## How to Make a Peach Fly

___ The 502 seagulls will lift the peach out of the water and fly away with it.

___ Use the Earthworm to lure a seagull.

_1_ Get Miss Spider and the Silkworm to spin silk strings.

___ Repeat steps 1–4 until you catch 502 seagulls.

___ As a seagull dives for the Earthworm, capture it with a silk string. Make sure you pull the Earthworm out of danger in time.

___ Tie the silk string to the peach stem.

Name _____

# Mystery Writing!

A friend was cutting out words to write a mystery note but fled before finishing. Find out what the friend was going to say. Add your own words to make each fragment into a complete sentence. Then put the sentences together and write your mystery note.

leaving on a trip

a million dollars

a tall man

*Friday night at seven o'clock*

a telephone booth

the captain

_____

_____

_____

_____

_____

_____

_____

_____

_____

..................................................................................................

Name

# What's the Ending?

For each word, write the base word and ending. Check a dictionary
if you are unsure about the spelling of a base word.

| | Base word | Ending |
|---|---|---|
| **1** fatter | | |
| **2** hurling | | |
| **3** cruises | | |
| **4** tethered | | |
| **5** zaniest | | |

Write the word from the chart that best completes each sentence.
(Hint: If you're not sure what the word means, the ending of the
word will help you place it in the right sentence.)

**6** When a shark is hungry, it _____

the waters in search of food.

**7** The sharks kept _____ themselves

at the peach.

**8** James thought the Earthworm would make good bait because

he was _____ than the others.

**9** The Earthworm thought James's plan was the

_____ idea he had ever heard.

**10** James caught a seagull and _____

it to the peach stem.

Name _____

# Dangerous Word Rescue

Find a word outside the peach that has the same, or almost the same, meaning as a word inside the peach. Draw a line connecting the two words.

_____

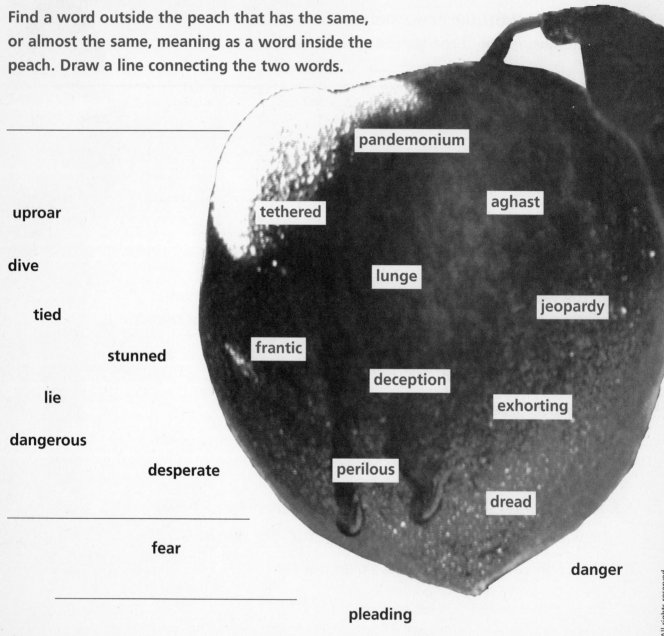

pandemonium

aghast

tethered

lunge

jeopardy

frantic

deception

exhorting

perilous

dread

uproar

dive

tied

stunned

lie

dangerous

desperate

_____

fear

danger

_____

pleading

_____

On each blank line, write another word that has a meaning similar to a word in the peach. Then connect your new word to its synonym.

# Make Waves

**Long *a* and Long *e***   Some Spelling Words have the long *a* sound, shown as |ā|. The |ā| sound can be spelled with the pattern *a*-consonant-*e*, *ai*, or *ay*.

|ā|   wake   bait   sway

The other Spelling Words have the long *e* sound, shown as |ē|. The |ē| sound can be spelled with the pattern *ea* or *ee*.

|ē|   peach   between

## Spelling Words

1. peach
2. bait
3. beast
4. between
5. afraid
6. wake
7. sway
8. scale
9. speed
10. stray

**My Study List**
What other words do you need to study for spelling? Add them to My Study List for *James and the Giant Peach* in the back of this book.

Write the Spelling Words that match the pattern for the long vowel sound shown on each wave.

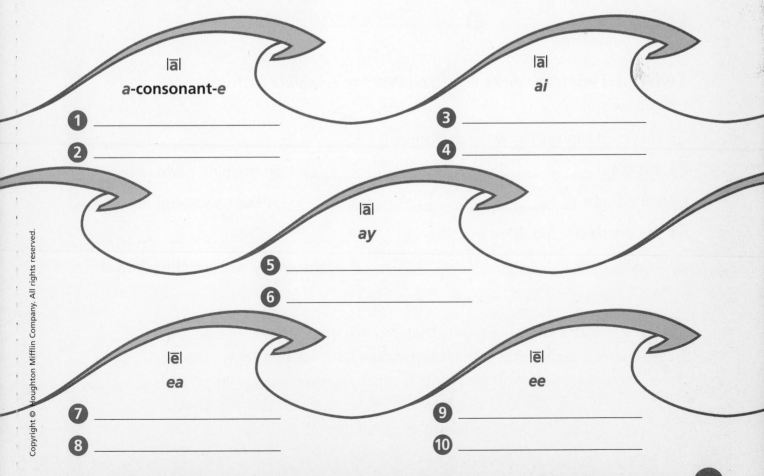

|ā|   *a*-consonant-*e*

1 _____
2 _____

|ā|   *ai*

3 _____
4 _____

|ā|   *ay*

5 _____
6 _____

|ē|   *ea*

7 _____
8 _____

|ē|   *ee*

9 _____
10 _____

Name

# Spelling Spree

**Proofreading** Circle five misspelled Spelling Words in this poem by Miss Spider. Then write each word correctly.

**Spelling Words**
1. peach
2. bait
3. beast
4. between
5. afraid
6. wake
7. sway
8. scale
9. speed
10. stray

We float on our peach betwen sky and sea,
So afrade when we start to swai.
And should a straye breeze
Make one of us sneeze,
A beest just might bite us today!

❶ _____   ❸ _____   ❺ _____
❷ _____   ❹ _____

**Twisted Twisters** Write a Spelling Word to complete each tongue twister.

❻ Silkwood spun string with spectacular _____.

❼ Put the _____ pit on the pink plate.

❽ Bill bought _____ at the boathouse on the bay.

❾ Set the six silk spools on the silver _____.

❿ We'll _____ the weary worm so he will work.

 **Peach Patrol** Imagine that you are floating over the sea on a giant peach. What is the weather like? Is it windy? Rainy? On a separate piece of paper, write a short weather report. Tell what the day is like. Also describe how the weather conditions will affect your trip. Use Spelling Words from the list.

# Soar with Seagulls

declarative

They are floating in the ocean.

interrogative

Are they on the peach?

imperative

Get away as fast as you can.

exclamatory

How clever they are!

**Kinds of Sentences** Read the seagulls' ads for their airline service. Write the correct end mark at the end of each sentence. Then name each sentence by writing *declarative, interrogative, imperative,* or *exclamatory* on each banner.

1. What a peachy ride you will have
   _____

2. Whistle when you are ready
   _____

3. We can take you anywhere
   _____

4. What are you waiting for
   _____

5. We promise a smooth flight
   _____

Name

# Get a Job!

**Kinds of Sentences** Help the animals get jobs. Write the name of a suitable job next to each animal, using jobs listed in the box or others. Then write a sentence the animal might say to "sell" itself. The label tells which kind of sentence to write.

butcher
window washer
tennis player
carpenter
firefighter
postal worker

| | |
|---|---|
| | Job _____<br><br>Declarative _____<br><br>_____ |
| | Job _____<br><br>Exclamatory _____<br><br>_____ |
| | Job _____<br><br>Declarative _____<br><br>_____ |
| | Job _____<br><br>Imperative _____<br><br>_____ |
| | Job _____<br><br>Exclamatory _____<br><br>_____ |

Name

# Rescue Diagram

**Draw a diagram that shows**

1. an explorer on one side of a wide <u>lead</u>
2. the rest of the <u>expedition</u> on the other side
3. some <u>sledges</u> and dog teams
4. an <u>ice floe</u> floating down the lead

How can the explorer use the ice floe to rejoin the expedition?

1. Add arrows to show the route the stranded explorer must take.

2. Add an <u>interpreter</u> translating your directions to the explorer.
   Write your directions in a speech balloon.

3. Then use the underlined words to label your diagram.

DIAGRAM

Name

# Following in Henson's Footsteps

**Answer each question. You may look back at the selection if you wish.**

**1** Why did Peary and Henson make six attempts to reach
the North Pole? _____

_____

_____

**2** What were some of Matt's responsibilities once the expedition arrived
at Cape Sheridan? _____

_____

_____

**3** What is an example of Henson using his survival skills to help
himself or another person? _____

_____

_____

**4** How did Matt feel when the expedition reached the North Pole? Why do you
think he felt that way? _____

_____

_____

**5** Which of Matthew Henson's qualities and abilities do you think
were most important? Why? _____

_____

_____

_____

Name

# Pack It Up!

Pack your bags for a trip to the Arctic. In the box are all the names
of items you'll need. Write each item name in the correct category.
When you've used all the words, you'll have finished packing.

| | |
|---|---|
| parka | bacon |
| mitten | pemmican |
| pickax | thermometer |
| shovel | walrus meat |
| bandages | compass |

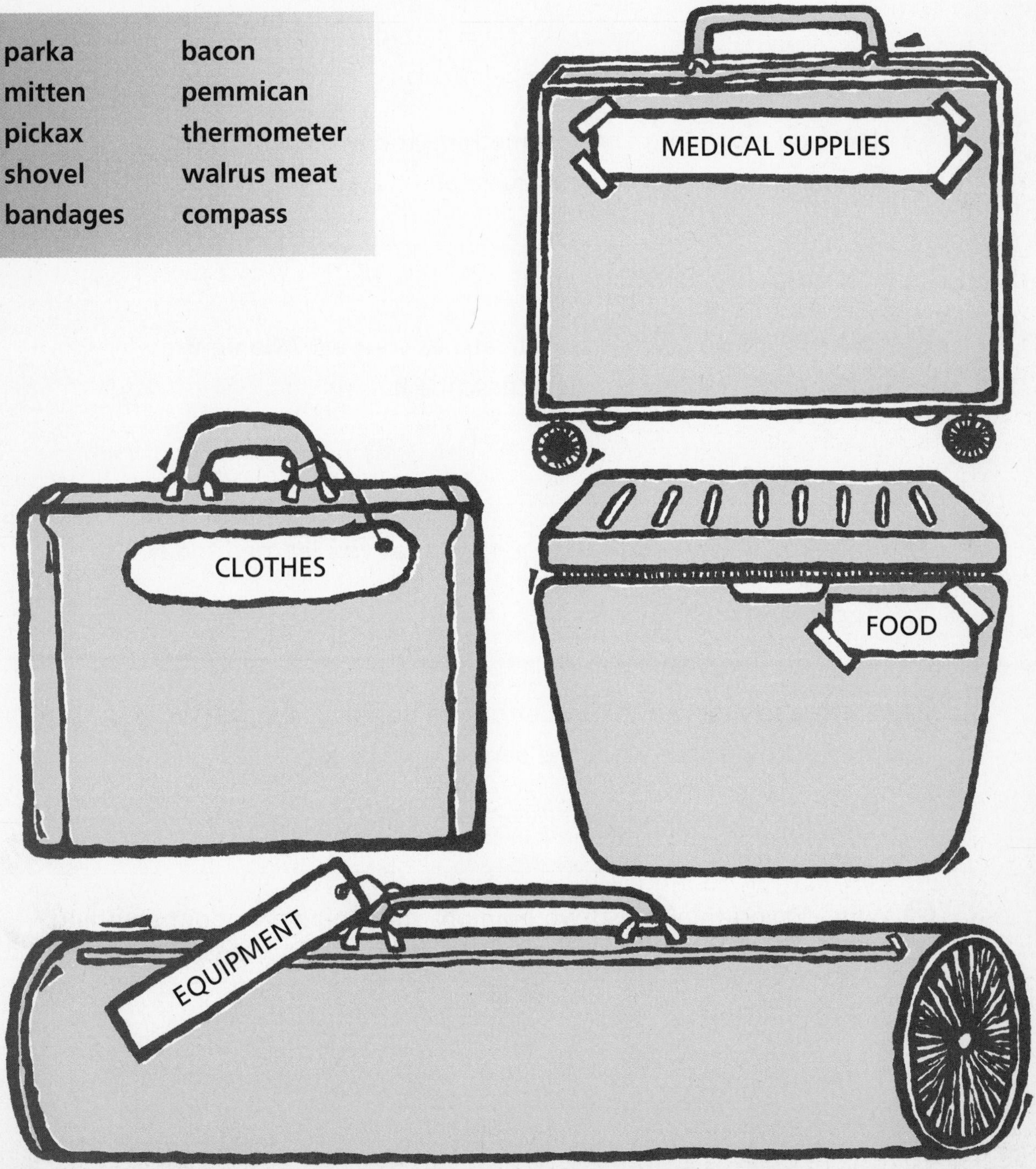

MEDICAL SUPPLIES

CLOTHES

FOOD

EQUIPMENT

Name

# Keeping a Journal

Matt Henson kept a journal of events in his life.  Answer these
questions.  Then use the answers to begin your own journal.

**1** Have you wondered about something today but not asked
anyone about it? Write your question.

_____

_____

**2** Look around you. What object catches your eye? Name the
object and list a few words to describe it.

_____

_____

**3** Write two new words, facts, or ideas that you learned today.

_____

_____

**4** Watch a stranger on the street or in a bus or in a store. Write
three details about what the person does or says.

_____

_____

**5** What do you think? List two opinions that you have about anything.

_____

_____

Name

# Igloo Words

Matthew Henson's igloo has words on it. Circle each word
with a suffix meaning "someone who." Then use
those words to complete the sentences.

typist

number

driver        sailor        sugar

list

biologist        commander        accordian

scholar        assist    under    error

musician        author        powder        anchor

poor

burglar        Italian        cover  twist  fist    under

**1** Marco is an _____ pilot from Rome.

**2** The bus _____ drops me off near my house.

**3** We caught a _____ climbing in the window.

**4** The _____ pulled up the ship's anchor.

**5** The navy _____ shouted orders.

**6** The _____ is conducting an experiment in the laboratory.

**7** Who is the _____ of that book?

**8** She is the fastest _____ in the office.

**9** The _____ is rehearsing with the orchestra.

**10** Good study habits will make you a better _____.

   Journey to Adventure!   **23**

Name ..............................................................................

# Who Am I?

Make up riddles to ask your classmates! Write the job
of your choice next to the question "Who am I?" Then
choose a word from each list to complete the clue
sentences. Each sentence should give a clue about
the job.

**TIP:** When you share your riddles, read only the clues.
Don't read the answer to the question "Who am I?"

**1** Who am I? _____

Clue: I am part of a(n) _____ .

Clue: I travel by _____ .

Clue: I work near a(n) _____ .

Who am I?

**2** Who am I? _____

Clue: I belong to a(n) _____ .

Clue: I take (a) _____ to work.

Clue: I see a(n) _____ where I work.

Who am I?

**Write your own clues!**

**3** Who am I? _____

Clue: _____

Clue: _____

Clue: _____

Who am I?

**Jobs**
interpreter
explorer
sailor
doctor

**Teams**
expedition
crew
medical practice
staff

**Transportation**
sledges
ship
airplane
train

**Surroundings**
ice floe
lead
office
playground

Name _____

# Safe Crossing

**Long *i* and Long *o*** Some Spelling Words have
the long *i* sound, shown as |ī|. The |ī| sound is often
spelled with the pattern *i*-consonant-*e* or *igh*.

|ī|    drive    sight

The other Spelling Words have the long *o* sound,
shown as |ō|. The |ō| sound is often spelled with
the pattern *o*-consonant-*e*, *oa*, or *ow*.

|ō|    froze    goal    snow

## Spelling Words

1. snow
2. goal
3. froze
4. sight
5. drive
6. wrote
7. load
8. midnight
9. prize
10. narrow

### My Study List
What other words do you
need to study for spelling?
Add them to My Study List for *Arctic
Explorer: The Story of Matthew
Henson* in the back of this book.

**Help Matt cross the ice to return to the ship. Write the Spelling
Words that match the spelling pattern shown on each block of ice.**

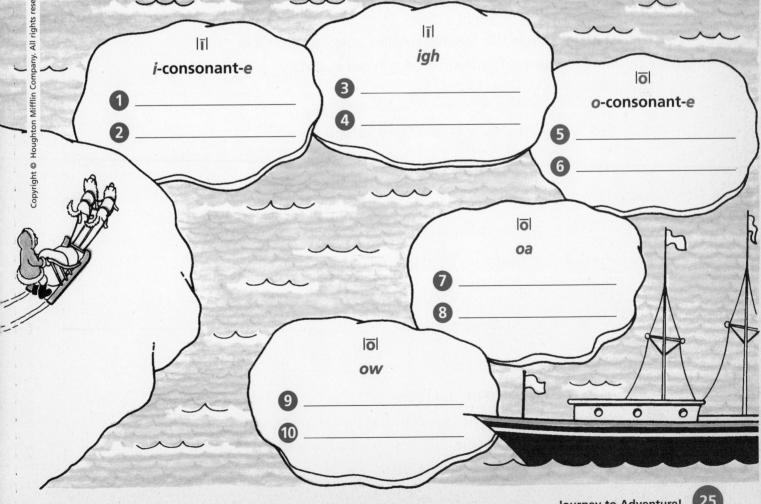

|ī|
*i*-consonant-*e*
1. _____
2. _____

|ī|
*igh*
3. _____
4. _____

|ō|
*o*-consonant-*e*
5. _____
6. _____

|ō|
*oa*
7. _____
8. _____

|ō|
*ow*
9. _____
10. _____

Name

# Spelling Spree

**Analogies** An **analogy** compares two pairs of
words. The words in the first pair are related to
each other in the same way as the words in the
second pair. Write a Spelling Word to complete
each analogy.

**Spelling Words**

1. snow
2. goal
3. froze
4. sight
5. drive
6. wrote
7. load
8. midnight
9. prize
10. narrow

**Example:** Water is to ice as rain is to _____ snow _____.

**1** Morning is to evening as noon is to _____.

**2** Present is to gift as award is to _____.

**3** Plane is to fly as car is to _____.

**4** Highway is to wide as path is to _____.

**5** Suitcase is to pack as moving van is to _____.

**Proofreading** Circle the five misspelled Spelling Words in
this explorer's log entry. Then write each word correctly.

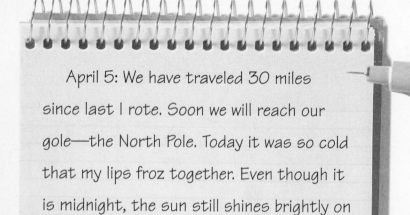

April 5: We have traveled 30 miles
since last I rote. Soon we will reach our
gole—the North Pole. Today it was so cold
that my lips froz together. Even though it
is midnight, the sun still shines brightly on
the sno. What an amazing sighte!

**6** _____

**7** _____

**8** _____

**9** _____

**10** _____

**Ask the Explorer** Imagine that you had the chance to
interview Matthew Henson. On a separate piece of paper, write
five questions that you might have asked about his journey.
Use Spelling Words from the list.

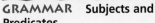
Name

# Bold Explorers

## Subjects and Predicates   A computer mixed up the predicates in the following paragraph.  In the left column, write the complete subjects.  In the right column, write the complete predicate that goes with each subject.

A growing dampness sniffed. The women in the expedition raised his nose to the scent of the coming danger. The dogs, the sleds, and the ice were not aware of the change. Some of the dogs was making the cold air heavy. One were demanding all their attention.

| SUBJECT | PREDICATE |
|---|---|
| **1** | |
| **2** | |
| **3** | |
| **4** | |
| **5** | |

Name

# Keep It Simple!

| SIMPLE SUBJECTS | | SIMPLE PREDICATES | |
|---|---|---|---|
| This brave | team | is heading | north. |
| | They | are | ready. |
| Captain Ramos | | waves. | |
| | (You) | Wish | them luck. |
| COMPLETE SUBJECTS | | COMPLETE PREDICATES | |

## Subjects and Predicates  Underline the simple subjects and the simple predicates. If the subject is understood, circle the sentence.

**1** Matt Henson will plant a flag.

**2** The ice split with a loud crack.

**3** They sledged in sunlight at night.

**4** Jump over the crack in the ice.

**5** The brave team had been gone for days.

**6** The route to the Pole is long, hard, and confusing.

**Write the simple subjects to complete this puzzle. The numbers in the puzzle match the sentences.**

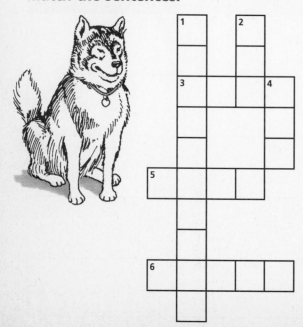

**Write the simple predicates to complete this puzzle. The numbers in the puzzle match the sentences**

1. _ _ _ _ _ _ ○

2. _ _ _ ○ _

3. _ _ ○ _ ○ _

4. _ ○ _

5. ○ _ _ _ _ ○ _

6. ○ _

**Unscramble the letters to tell when Peary and Henson often traveled.**

The secret word is _____.

# In My Opinion

What do you have opinions about?  Does one of these topics spark
a reaction?

## Topics for a Personal Essay

| | | |
|---|---|---|
| Winning and Losing | Eating | My Favorite Holiday |
| Clothing Fads | Life in the City/Country | Rain |
| Being Female/Male | Report Cards | What Makes Me Angry |
| Fairness | What's Important to Me | |

## My Personal Essay Topics

**Write five topics that you have opinions about.**

_____

_____

_____

_____

_____

**Think about each topic you wrote. Ask yourself these questions.**

Would I enjoy writing
about this?

Do I have enough
to say?

Can I think of
good examples to
make my
thoughts clear?

**Circle the topic you will write about.**

# Your Thoughts, Please

Complete the idea map to show your focus idea, the thoughts about it, and examples that you can use.

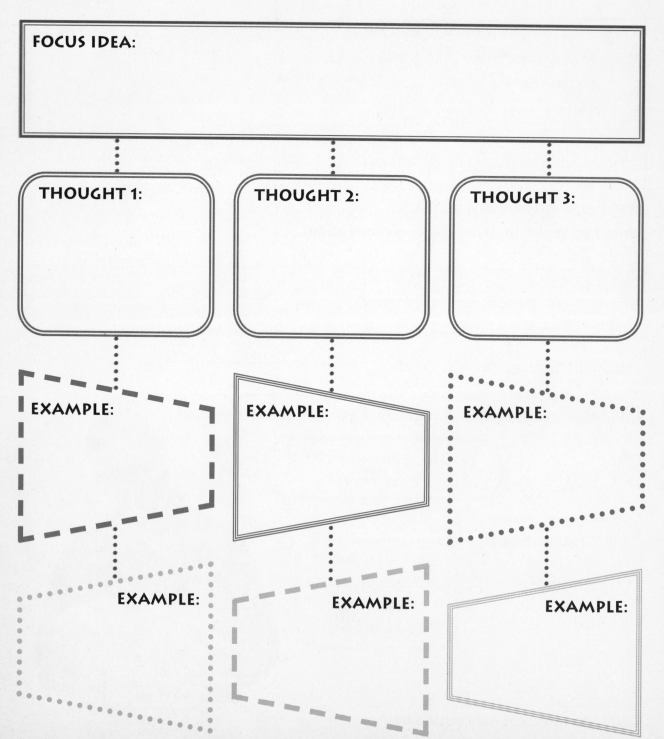

**FOCUS IDEA:**

**THOUGHT 1:**

**THOUGHT 2:**

**THOUGHT 3:**

**EXAMPLE:**

**EXAMPLE:**

**EXAMPLE:**

**EXAMPLE:**

**EXAMPLE:**

**EXAMPLE:**

Name _____

# Making It Better

Reread your essay to yourself and make changes, using the Revising Checklist. Then use the Questions for a Writing Conference to help you discuss your essay with a classmate.

## Revising Checklist

☐ Did I state my focus idea clearly?

☐ Do all my points, thoughts, and examples relate to my focus idea?

☐ Is each point or thought treated clearly and separately?

☐ Did I give an example to support each point or thought? Could I give better ones?

## Questions for a Writing Conference

- What is the best part?
- Is the opening interesting?
- Is the focus idea clearly presented?
- Do all of the ideas keep to the focus?
- Are related thoughts and examples grouped together?
- Are more or different examples needed?
- What parts are unclear?
- Does the closing make the essay seem finished?

Write notes to remember ideas discussed in your writing conference.

### My Notes

_____

_____

_____

_____

_____

_____

_____

_____

Name _____

# Mission to Mars

Use these space words to complete the space log entry.

atmosphere    gravity    orbit    meteorites    comet    particles

Stardate: December 1, 2053

Mission: To explore Mars

After months of traveling, we have finally spotted Mars. The planet is still a distance away, but already the spacecraft is being pulled by Mars's _____. Within a few days we will begin our _____ of the planet. We will circle Mars ten times before we land on its surface.

Once we land, we'll explore the planet. My first job is to collect rocks. With luck, I'll find some _____. They are _____ of rock that have fallen from outer space. My other job is to set up a telescope to view the glowing tail of a _____ as it flies by Mars.

We'll have to wear space suits while we're walking on the planet. The _____ of Mars has very little oxygen, and we wouldn't be able to breathe otherwise.

Name

# Space Profiles

Complete these profiles of *Voyager*
and the planets.

Saturn has

thousands of rings

made up of

_____

_____. Saturn's largest moon is called

_____.

*Voyager 1*

and *Voyager 2* were

launched in 1977 to

study _____

_____

_____. *Voyager 1* visited

and photographed _____

_____. *Voyager 2* traveled

to Jupiter, Saturn, Uranus, and Neptune.

Uranus is _____

_____

_____ in color. Scientists think that

_____

_____ hold one of Uranus's rings together.

In size, Jupiter
is the

_____

in the solar system. Jupiter has a mark
on its surface called _____

_____ of all the planets

_____.

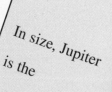

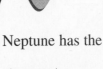

Neptune has the

strongest

_____ measured on any

planet. Neptune's moon Triton has streaks

on its icy surface. The streaks are caused by

_____

_____.

Name _____

# One Giant Leap!

Label each part of the article with a word from the box. Then answer the question.

> graphic aid
> heading
> caption
> introduction

*On July 20, 1969, Neil A. Armstrong made history by being the first human to walk on the moon. As Armstrong stepped from his* Apollo 11 *lunar module he said, "That's one small step for a man, one giant leap for mankind." This article will examine, in the order they happened, the many "baby" steps that were important for the success of the* Apollo 11 *mission.*

**1** _____

## Blast Off!

The mission began on the morning of July 16, 1969. At 9:32 A.M. the earth shook as the *Apollo 11*'s Saturn 5 rocket ignited. More than seven million pounds of thrust heaved the spacecraft off the launch pad. In the command module atop the rocket, astronauts Neil A. Armstrong, Michael Collins, and Edwin E. Aldrin, Jr. nervously waited.

**2** _____

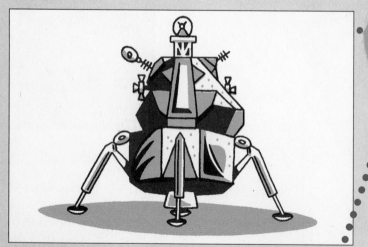

**3** _____

**4** _____

**5** How does the introduction say the article is organized?

_____

_____

_____

**When the astronauts returned to Earth, the landing craft's descent stage was left on the moon.**

Name

# Alike and Different

Use this graphic organizer to plan your paragraphs of
comparison and contrast. Write the name of one of the objects you are
comparing in one of the circles. Under each name, list the ways in which that object
is different from the other one. In the space where the circles overlap,
list the ways the objects are alike.

**Object**                                    **Object**

# Categorically Speaking

**What category fits each list? Write the category names above the lists. Then add at least one more word to each list.**

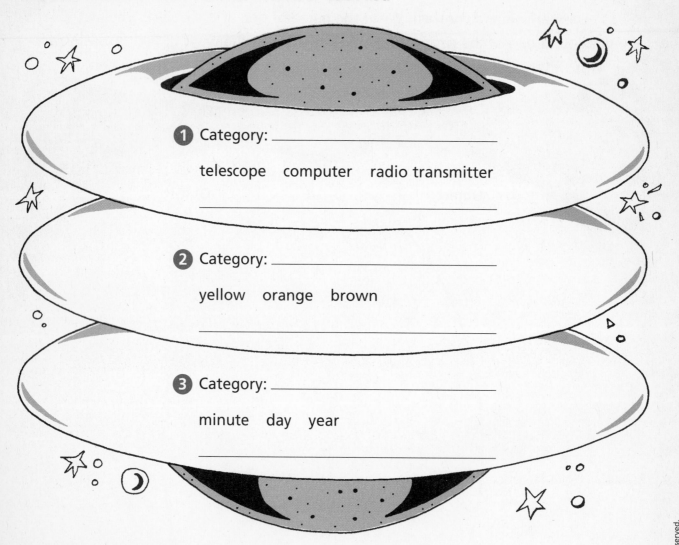

**1** Category: _____

telescope   computer   radio transmitter

_____

**2** Category: _____

yellow   orange   brown

_____

**3** Category: _____

minute   day   year

_____

**Circle the word that does not belong in each category. Then tell why it does not belong.**

**4** river      mountain      lake      pond

_____

**5** Spain      Australia      California      Mexico

_____

Name _____

# Blue (and Red and Green) Moons

Draw a picture of one moon that you've read about. Label some of the features of your drawing. Features might include **meteorites, craters, geysers,** and **volcanoes.**

Name of Moon: _____

Write a description of the moon. Use these words in your description: **gravity, atmosphere, orbit, particles, comet,** and **asteroid.**

_____

_____

_____

_____

........................................................

Name

# Voyage to the Stars

**Long *u***  Each Spelling Word has the long *u* sound. This sound can be said two ways, as in *huge* and *blue.* The long *u* sound you hear in *huge* is shown as |yo͞o|. The long *u* sound you hear in *blue* is shown as |o͞o|. The |yo͞o| and |o͞o| sounds are often spelled with the pattern *u*-consonant-*e*, *ue*, *oo*, *ui*, or *ou*.

|yo͞o| or |o͞o|    huge  blue  smooth  juice  group

Write each Spelling Word beneath the matching pattern.

## Spelling Words

1. huge
2. blue
3. smooth
4. clue
5. ooze
6. group
7. juice
8. route
9. rude
10. bruise

**My Study List**
What other words do you need to study for spelling? Add them to My Study List for *Voyager: An Adventure to the Edge of the Solar System* in the back of this book.

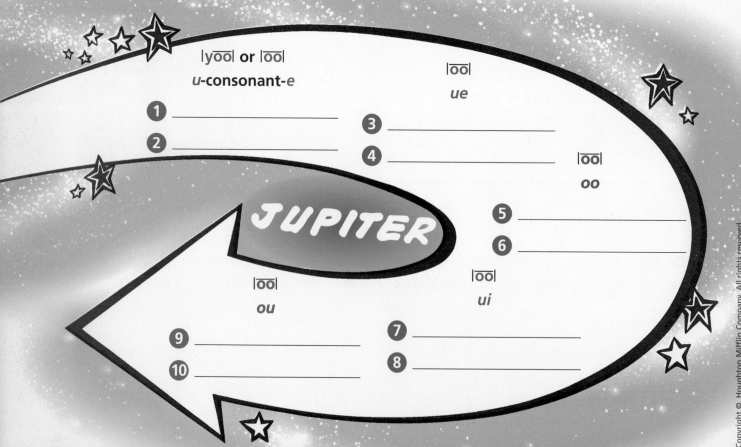

|yo͞o| or |o͞o|
*u*-consonant-*e*

1. _____
2. _____

|o͞o|
*ue*

3. _____
4. _____

|o͞o|
*oo*

5. _____
6. _____

|o͞o|
*ou*

9. _____
10. _____

|o͞o|
*ui*

7. _____
8. _____

JUPITER

Name _____

# Spelling Spree

**Across the Universe**  Write the Spelling Word
that fits each clue.

## Spelling Words

1. huge
2. blue
3. smooth
4. clue
5. ooze
6. group
7. juice
8. route
9. rude
10. bruise

**Across**

4. more than two
   people or things
5. what a detective
   looks for
6. not polite

**Down**

1. a black eye is one
2. what you squeeze
   from an orange
3. a color of the sky

## Proofreading  Find and circle four
misspelled Spelling Words in this
description of a prize in the distant
future. Then write each word correctly.

**7** _____

**8** _____

**9** _____

**10** _____

Here's what you've won—a trip to
Jupiter! Follow the rute *Voyager I* took
past the smoothe, blue surface of
Europa, one of Jupiter's moons.
Watch lava ooz over Io's surface.
Then gasp as the gas giant itself
comes into view, with its huje red
spot and many colors. You'll live a
lifetime of thrills in just one day!

**Over and Out**  Imagine that you are the pilot of the first
mission to Neptune. You are seeing sights previously seen only by
*Voyager*'s cameras. On a separate piece of paper, write a dialogue
you might have with Mission Control. Describe where you are, what
you are seeing, and how you feel. Use Spelling Words from the list.

Name

# Robot Connections

**Run-on:**
Astronauts could not travel to Neptune a robot spacecraft could.

**Correct:**
Astronauts could not travel to Neptune. A robot spacecraft could.

**Correct:**
Astronauts could not travel to Neptune, but a robot spacecraft could.

## Correcting Run-on Sentences  A robot spacecraft has beamed back information about newly discovered planets, but the robot uses run-on sentences. Write the run-on sentences correctly.

**1** This planet has a huge red spot the spot seems fiery.

_____

_____

_____

**2** Moons circle this planet nine were identified.

_____

_____

**3** This planet appears very stormy a closer look is needed.

_____

_____

**4** Could this planet have forests there are many large, green areas.

_____

_____

**5** What an amazing planet this is tiny lights sparkle all over it.

_____

_____

**6** Does this planet have mountains with clouds overhead does it have erupting volcanoes?

_____

_____

_____

Name

# Message from Space

## Correcting Run-on Sentences This paragraph has been
sent directly from space as one long run-on sentence. Help the
scientist read it by writing it correctly.

> United States scientists have sent several spacecraft to
> Mars in 1964 Mariner IV was launched it sent back the first
> pictures of the planet some Mariners flew by Mars one
> orbited the planet for about a year two Viking spacecraft
> actually landed on Mars in 1976 they studied the planet for
> over four years they collected information about its
> atmosphere and surface much has been learned about our
> neighboring planet there are still many unanswered
> questions.

_____

_____

_____

_____

_____

_____

_____

_____

_____

_____

_____

_____

_____

_____

Name

# Planning an Expedition

Plan an expedition to one of the planets or moons described
in *Voyager* to collect samples of what you find there.

| Planet I will visit | |
|---|---|
| Special challenges I will face on this planet | |
| Equipment I will need to travel to and from the planet | |
| Equipment I will need for survival | |
| Equipment I will need to collect samples | |

List six important stages or events in your expedition plan.
Your list should include examples of these categories:
**Travel, Survival, and Collecting Samples.**

**1** _____

**2** _____

**3** _____

**4** _____

**5** _____

**6** _____

Create drawings and descriptions
showing each stage or event. Use your
drawings to present your expedition
plan to your classmates. Use the
checklist to be sure you are ready to
present your plan.

## Checklist

❑ My drawings and presentation show how to
meet the special challenges of this planet.

❑ My drawings show how I will travel, survive,
and collect samples.

❑ My drawings are organized in the correct
sequence.

Name

# In the Wild

After reading each selection, complete the chart below and on the next page to show what you discovered.

| | Wolves | The Midnight Fox | Adiós falcón/ Good-bye, Falcon |
|---|---|---|---|
| **What kind of writing is the selection an example of?** | | | |
| **What do you think are the author's feelings about wildlife?** | | | |
| **What problems do the animals face? How are they resolved?** | | | |

Name

# In the Wild

After reading each selection, complete the chart
to show what you discovered.

|  | Wolves | The Midnight Fox | Adiós falcón/ Good-bye, Falcon |
|---|---|---|---|
| What ideas about wildlife preservation are raised in this selection? |  |  |  |
| How do you feel about the animals in the selection? |  |  |  |

What have you learned in this theme about preserving wildlife?

_____

_____

_____

_____

Name

# Tracking Down Definitions

Track down the definitions for the vocabulary words.  Draw a line
from each word to its definition.

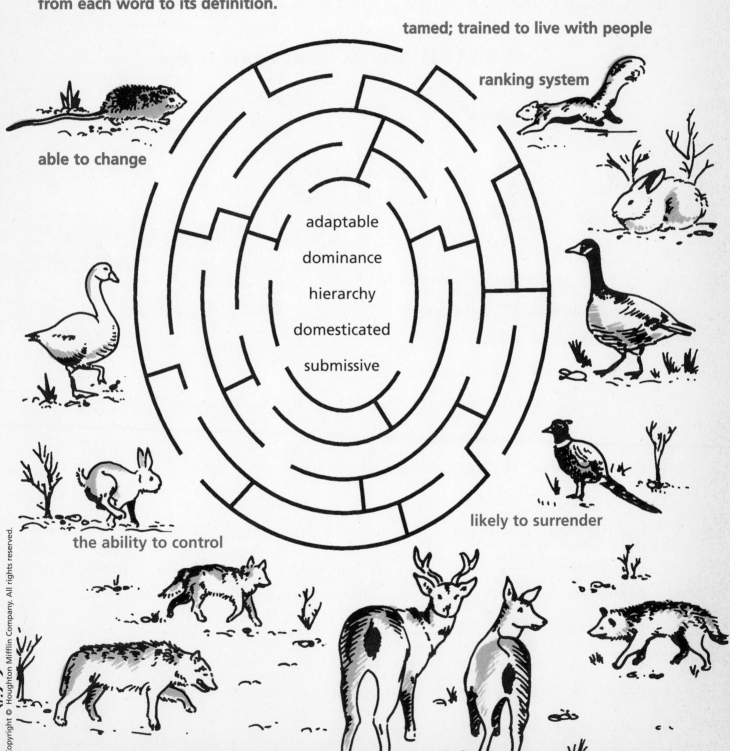

tamed; trained to live with people

ranking system

able to change

adaptable

dominance

hierarchy

domesticated

submissive

likely to surrender

the ability to control

Name

# Wanted: More Wolves!

Use what you've learned about wolves to complete
this "wanted" poster.

## WANTED: Wolves, alias *Canis lupus*

Description: Wolves look like _____

_____

Reputation: Many frightening stories and legends describe wolves as being _____

_____

Closest Relatives: The wolf's closest relatives are _____

_____

Lifestyle: Wolves live in packs. Pack leaders are called _____

_____

Range: Wolves once lived across much of the Northern Hemisphere. Now wolves

can be found mostly in _____

_____

Reason for Disappearance: Wolves have become endangered because _____

_____

# Get the Facts

Decide whether the sentences in bold are statements of fact or
statements expressing opinions. Then write **F** for fact or **O** for
opinion on the lines.

# The Key Deer

Just a few years ago, Big Pine
Key was a rural crossroads with a
population of only 1500. **But times
have changed for the worse on
these sunny islands off the
southern tip of Florida. Now Big
Pine Key has a population of
over 3000.** A shopping mall and
sprawling neighborhoods have
replaced its beautiful pine forests
and palm trees.

But Big Pine Key is in danger of
losing some of its unique wildlife as
well. **The islands are the last
home of the endangered key
deer. Today there are fewer
than 300 of the deer left.** The
deer, which grow no bigger than the
average dog, need the shelter and
food that the forests provide.

**Wildlife is a precious
resource.** Should we search for
ways to protect our precious
wildlife? **We must decide now.**
Soon there may be no key deer left.

What do you think is the writer's viewpoint?

_____

_____

_____

_____

Name

# Plan Ahead

Use this page to plan your book report. Then write your report on a separate sheet of paper.

Title:

Author:

Fiction or Nonfiction:

Setting:

Main Character(s):

What is the book about?

What is your favorite part of the book?

Do you like this book? Why or why not?

Name

# Howl!

**Match the correct definition to the boldface word.
Then write the homophone pairs under the wolves.**

_____ 1. The wolf followed the **scent** of the moose.

_____ 2. Wolves have long, bushy **tails.**

_____ 3. The gray wolf **won** the fight.

_____ 4. Water runs off wolf fur the **way** it runs off a raincoat.

_____ 5. That fuzzy pup is only **one** week old.

_____ 6. The sound of shots **sent** the wolves running.

_____ 7. How much does an average wolf **weigh?**

_____ 8. Baby wolves can't eat **meat** right away.

_____ 9. Many nursery **tales** describe wolves as being sly.

_____ 10. Would you be afraid to **meet** a wolf?

a. gained victory

b. animal flesh used as food

c. manner of doing something

d. to come in contact with

e. caused to move or go

f. parts of animals' bodies

g. the trail of a hunted animal

h. to have a particular heaviness

i. stories

j. the number before two

 **11**    **13** _____   **15** _____

_____   _____   _____

 **12**    **14** _____

_____   _____

Name

# Track of the Wolf

Write the vocabulary word that completes each sentence.
Then use the letters that the wolf tracks touch to complete
the sentence describing wolves.

| adaptable | domesticated | prey | dominance |
| traits | hybrid | hierarchy | submissive |

**1** Ranking of wolves in a pack
is called ____.

\_\_ \_\_ \_\_ \_\_ \_\_ \_\_ \_\_ \_\_ \_\_

**2** Lower-ranked wolves are
____ to higher-ranked
wolves.

\_\_ \_\_ \_\_ \_\_ \_\_ \_\_ \_\_ \_\_ \_\_ \_\_

**3** Alpha wolves have ____ over
the other wolves in the pack.

\_\_ \_\_ \_\_ \_\_ \_\_ \_\_ \_\_ \_\_ \_\_

**4** Wolves make bad pets
because they aren't ____.

\_\_ \_\_ \_\_ \_\_ \_\_ \_\_ \_\_ \_\_ \_\_ \_\_ \_\_ \_\_

**5** Wolves survive in different
climates because they are
____.

\_\_ \_\_ \_\_ \_\_ \_\_ \_\_ \_\_ \_\_ \_\_

**6** The red wolf might be a ____
of the wolf and the coyote.

\_\_ \_\_ \_\_ \_\_ \_\_ \_\_

**7** Wolves hunt in packs to
catch larger ____ such as
moose or elk.

\_\_ \_\_ \_\_ \_\_

**8** Wolves and dogs share many
of the same ____.

\_\_ \_\_ \_\_ \_\_ \_\_ \_\_

**Wolves**     \_\_ \_\_ \_\_   \_\_ \_\_ \_\_ \_\_ \_\_ \_\_ .

Name

# Haunting Howls

**Vowel + *r* Sounds** Some Spelling Words have the vowel + *r* sounds that you hear in *bare.* These sounds, shown as lârl, are close to the lāl sound. The lârl sounds are often spelled with the patterns *are* and *air*.

lârl   b**are**   h**air**

The other Spelling Words have the vowel + *r* sounds that you hear in *sharp*. These sounds, shown as lärl, are close to the läl sound. The lärl sounds are usually spelled with the pattern *ar*.

lärl   sh**arp**

## Spelling Words

1. sharp
2. bark
3. hair
4. bare
5. startle
6. pair
7. care
8. share
9. apart
10. stare

**My Study List**
What other words do you need to study for spelling? Add them to My Study List for *Wolves* in the back of this book.

Write each Spelling Word under the wolf with the correct sounds and spelling pattern.

lârl   **are**

1. _____
2. _____
3. _____
4. _____

lârl   **air**

5. _____
6. _____

lärl   **ar**

7. _____
8. _____
9. _____
10. _____

Name

# Spelling Spree

**Wolf Words**  Write the Spelling Word that fits each clue.

1  surprise or alarm   __ __ __ __ __ ○ __

2  set of two matched things, such as shoes   __ __ ○ __

3  not together; in pieces   __ __ __ __ ○ __

4  gaze at steadily   __ ○ __ __ __

5  give help or keep safe   __ __ __ ○

6  not dull   __ __ __ ○ __

Now write the letters from the circles in order. This word names a group of wolf pups born at once to the same mother.

**Mystery Word:**  __ __ __ __ __ __

**Proofreading**  Find and circle four misspelled Spelling Words in this magazine article.  Then write each word correctly.

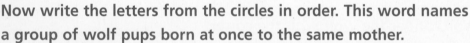

My dog Shep and I have had our shar of adventures.  Once we were hiking along a mountain trail.  Suddenly, Shep began to barck.  The hare on my neck stood up when Shep started to bair his teeth.  Just then a pair of wolves began howling, not ten feet away!  I sprinted for the car, but Shep beat me there by a mile!

7  _____

8  _____

9  _____

10  _____

**Howling Hits**  As a songwriter, you hope to raise money to save the wolves. On separate paper, write the titles of four "wolf" songs to include on your next album. Use capital letters to begin the first, last, and each important word in the title. Use Spelling Words from the list.

# Plural Puzzle Play

| Singular | pack | ranch | body | valley | silo | tomato | woman | elk |
|----------|------|-------|------|--------|------|--------|-------|-----|
| Plural | packs | ranches | bodies | valleys | silos | tomatoes | women | elk |

## Singular and Plural Nouns Complete the puzzle by writing the plural form of each singular noun. Use a dictionary if you need help.

**Across**

**1.** coyote

**7.** bush

**8.** trout

**9.** turkey

**11.** baby

**14.** foot

**15.** glass

**16.** hero

**17.** personality

**Down**

**1.** cage

**2.** year

**3.** trait

**4.** joy

**5.** path

**6.** wolf

**7.** birch

**10.** rodeo

**12.** arm

**13.** eye

**15.** goose

Name

# Animal Park Plurals

**Singular and Plural Nouns** Complete the signs by writing the plural form of each animal's name. Use a dictionary if you are unsure how to form the plural.

1. wallaby
2. reindeer
3. dingo
4. ox
5. panda
6. ostrich
7. donkey/burro
8. penguin

**How Do I Get There?** On another sheet of paper, write instructions telling how to get from the front gate of the animal park to the food stand. Be exact. Be sure to include the names of all the animals you would walk by.

Name

# Odd Word Out

Draw a line through the word that does not belong in each group. Write why the other three words belong together. The first one has been done for you.

| | |
|---|---|
| urgent | ~~cautious~~ |
| desperate | frantic |

**Example:** All but cautious mean "insistent; demanding attention."

| | |
|---|---|
| depressed | gloomy |
| discouraged | cheerful |

**1** _____

_____

| | |
|---|---|
| dread | terror |
| courage | apprehension |

**2** _____

_____

| | |
|---|---|
| calmly | anxiously |
| worriedly | uneasily |

**3** _____

_____

| | |
|---|---|
| doomed | condemned |
| fortunate | ill-fated |

**4** _____

_____

| | |
|---|---|
| despair | hopelessness |
| glee | powerlessness |

**5** _____

_____

Name _____

# Foxy Falsehoods

Mark a **T** if the statement is true and an **F** if it is false. If the statement is false, correct it to make a true statement.

**1** _____ Tom is spending the summer at Uncle Fred and Aunt Hazeline's farm.

_____

**2** _____ You can tell from reading the story that Uncle Fred probably has hunted foxes before.

_____

**3** _____ Tom wants Uncle Fred to find the den.

_____

**4** _____ Happ finds the fox's scent and leads Uncle Fred to the den.

_____

**5** _____ Tom is overjoyed when Uncle Fred finds the den.

_____

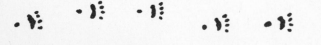

**Answer each question.**

**6** Why do you think Tom closes his eyes when Uncle Fred digs for

the baby fox?_____

_____

**7** Why does Aunt Millie feel better by the end of the story?

_____

_____

_____

# What Are They Like?

Complete the chart to tell what the characters in *The Midnight Fox* are like. You may look back at the selection if you wish.

| Character | What character says, does, or thinks | What you can infer about the character |
|---|---|---|
| Uncle Fred | He tells Tom, "Don't be in too big a hurry. Let's look a bit." | |
| Tom | Inside he's screaming, "You're burning up." | |
| Aunt Millie | She tells Tom not to be too late. When she sees that his face is red, she asks him if he's all right. Then she says Hazeline can take the shovel to her dad. | |
| Tom | He closes his eyes and presses his hands against his eyelids when Uncle Fred begins digging. | |

Name _____

# Foxy Facts

## Compound Sentences Revise this report on foxes to combine and vary the length of the sentences. Use commas and conjunctions.

Foxes live in farmlands and forests.  Their dens may be underground.  They may be in hollow trees.  Foxes rely on their highly developed senses for survival.  They watch for traps with their remarkable eyesight.  Their keen hearing picks up a mouse squeak from over one hundred feet away!  Baby foxes are called different names.  They can be called pups.  They can be called cubs.  The size of a fox litter varies.  Red foxes have from four to nine pups at a time.  Gray foxes have from three to five pups.  Foxes make farmers angry by eating their chickens.  They help farmers by eating mice and rats.

# Hunting for Suffixes

**Circle the words with the suffixes *-ful*, *-less*, and *-ly*
in the fox trail. Use the circled words to complete
the story.**

nlewkrunadrojsitirexcitedlyetryetfearlessshortyphappeacefulovinyouthappilyellowhatskillfulighoppractigracefulivelicyeswiftlyearlinelipdopelessadl

It was daybreak, and the forest was

_____. But not for long!  A shot

rang out.  The sleeping fox woke up and began

running _____ through the

forest.  Hunting dogs smelled the fox and

barked _____. But the

_____ fox knew how to

outsmart them!  He made _____

leaps into the air, backtracked, and ran through

water to make them lose the scent.  He wasn't

at all afraid. He was _____! The

hunters knew it was _____ and

gave up the chase. The fox seemed to smile

_____ as he watched them go.

Name

# Frantic Fox Frenzy

Read the sentences. If the underlined word is used correctly, color the egg. If not, use the correct word from the box to rewrite the sentence at the bottom.

| hopelessness | feeble | discouraged | dread | desperate | ecstatic |
|---|---|---|---|---|---|

**1** Anne knew the fox was in the hen house, so she opened the door <u>anxiously</u>. ◯

**2** She was <u>overjoyed</u> when she saw that three of her favorite hens had disappeared. ◯

**3** When Anne noticed that five other hens were missing, she was filled with <u>unconcern</u>. ◯

**4** She was certain a fox was stealing the hens. Unless she could capture the fox, she knew the <u>hopefulness</u> of the situation. ◯

**5** When the frightened fox saw Anne, a <u>satisfied</u> look flashed across his eyes. ◯

**6** The fox had no way to escape—he knew he was <u>doomed</u>. ◯

# Fox Trot

Name

**More Vowel + *r* Sounds** Some Spelling
Words have the vowel + *r* sounds that you hear in
*before*. These sounds, shown as |ôr|, are close to
the |ō| sound. The |ôr| sounds are often spelled
with the patterns *or*, *ore*, and *oar*.

|ôr|    porch    before    roar

The other Spelling Words have the vowel + *r*
sounds that you hear in *fear*. These sounds,
shown as |îr|, are close to the |ē| sound. The |îr|
sounds are often spelled with the patterns *eer* and *ear*.

|îr|    peer    fear

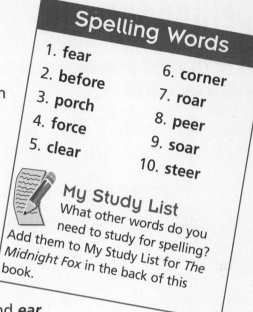

## Spelling Words

1. fear
2. before
3. porch
4. force
5. clear
6. corner
7. roar
8. peer
9. soar
10. steer

## My Study List
What other words do you
need to study for spelling?
Add them to My Study List for *The
Midnight Fox* in the back of this
book.

**Follow the fox. Write each Spelling Word next to the
paw print with the correct sounds and spelling pattern.**

|ôr| or

1 _____
2 _____
3 _____

|ôr| oar

4 _____
5 _____

|îr| ear

6 _____
7 _____

|ôr| ore

8 _____

|îr| eer

9 _____
10 _____

Name

# Spelling Spree

**Foxes in Boxes** Write the Spelling Word that answers each question.

### Spelling Words

1. fear
2. before
3. porch
4. force
5. clear
6. corner
7. roar
8. peer
9. soar
10. steer

1. Which word means "easy to see, hear, or understand"?

2. How do you make a bicycle turn right or left?

3. What word means the opposite of *weakness*?

4. What is another word for *glide* or *fly high*?

5. What can you sit on at the front, side, or back of a house?

6. What sound does an angry lion make?

1 _____
2 _____
3 _____
4 _____
5 _____
6 _____

**Proofreading** Find and circle four misspelled Spelling Words in these notes by a nature photographer. Then write each word correctly.

7. Set up the camera on the cornor of the cabin porch, where the view is clear.

8. Get shots of fox babies as they pere out from under a bush.

9. Film them befour they eat; they often nap afterwards.

10. Do not shout or make sudden moves. Otherwise, they'll feer the camera.

7 _____

9 _____

8 _____

10 _____

**Animal's Eye View** Imagine that you are a wild animal. Are you a fox stealing chickens? A raccoon raiding garbage cans? A wolf hunting for food? How do you view people and the way they treat your kind? State your opinion in a brief paragraph. Include at least three reasons why you think as you do. Use Spelling Words from the list.

# Trail Guide

Singular Possessives

A man's hat is in front of
the fox's den.

Plural Possessives

The men's hats are in
front of the foxes' den.

home of a porcupine
den of the fox
tracks of a deer
lodge of the beavers
playground of the
   squirrels
cave of the bats
honks of the geese
cocoons of the
   butterflies
call of the chickadee

**Possessive Nouns** Use the trail guide to complete
the sentences. For each stop on the trail, find the phrase
in the box that tells what to see. Rewrite the phrase,
using a possessive noun.

**Example:** The whole forest is the squirrels' playground.

**1** Look for the _____
   just beyond the bramble bushes.

**2** If you listen carefully, you might hear the
   _____.

**3** Notice the _____
   at the edge of the field.

**4** Look across the marsh to see the
   _____.

**5** Listen for the _____.

**6** This hollow log is a _____.

**7** Keep your eyes open for
   _____ on branches.

**8** You may spot a _____
   near the pond.

Name

# Creature Features

**Possessive Nouns**  What a strange animal you just saw in the woods! Match each phrase to its place on the animal. On the line next to the feature, rewrite the phrase, using a possessive noun. One label has been done. Draw one animal feature of your own on this creature and label it.

| |
|---|
| spots of a leopard |
| mane of a lion |
| wings of a bat |
| tusks of a walrus |
| antlers of two moose |
| hoofs of a horse |
| tails of two lizards |
| pouch of a kangaroo |

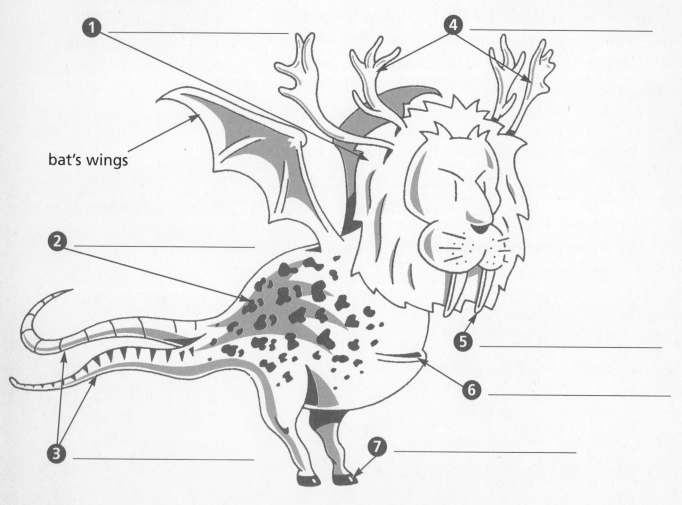

bat's wings

**Create Your Own Creature** On a separate sheet of paper, draw another creature made of different animal parts. Write phrases using possessive nouns to describe its features. Have a classmate try to identify the parts.

Name _____

# Be Persuasive

**Does one of these topics get you thinking?**

## TOPIC IDEAS

Persuade the owner of a computer store to sponsor a computer club

Persuade an author to speak to the class

Persuade the owner of a movie theater to build a wheelchair ramp

Persuade other students to help with a charity fund-raising event

Persuade the town council to pass a leash law

Persuade the physical education teacher to start a girls' soccer team

## My Ideas

Write five ideas that you have for persuading someone to do something. Next to each idea, write the audience you need to persuade.

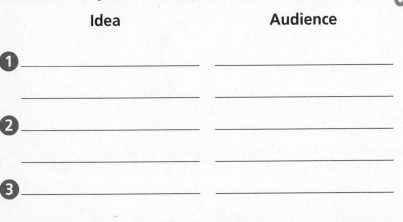

Do I know enough about this?

Can I give strong reasons with facts and examples?

Do I feel strongly about this?

Can I reach an audience who can make this happen?

| Idea | Audience |
|------|----------|
| **1** _____ | _____ |
| **2** _____ | _____ |
| **3** _____ | _____ |
| **4** _____ | _____ |
| **5** _____ | _____ |

**Ask yourself these questions about each idea. Then circle the topic that you will write about.**

# Prepare to Persuade

Fill in the persuasion map. Write your opinion and your goal—
what you want your audience to do. Then list your reasons and
the supporting facts and examples that you will use.

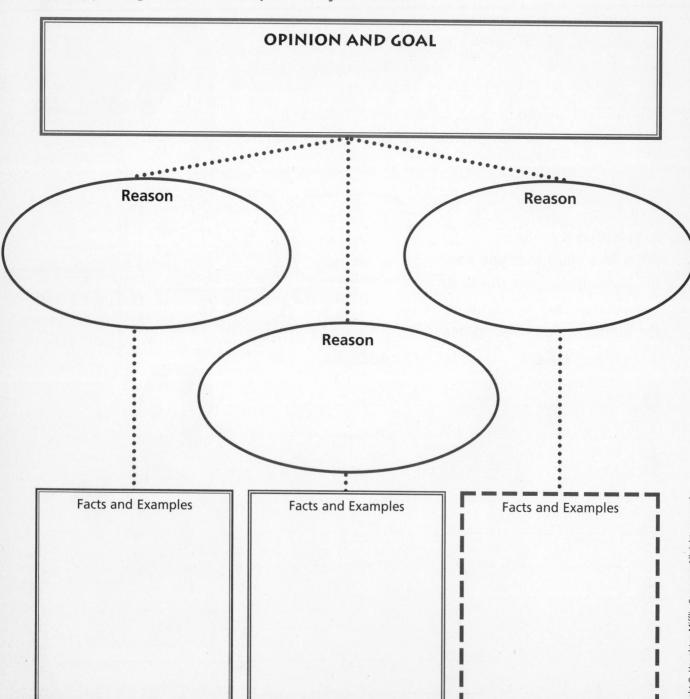

**OPINION AND GOAL**

Reason

Reason

Reason

Facts and Examples

Facts and Examples

Facts and Examples

Name

# Perfect Persuasion

Reread and revise your persuasive argument, using the Revising
Checklist. Then use the Questions for a Writing Conference to
discuss your paper with a classmate.

## Revising Checklist

❑  Did I state my opinion clearly?

❑  Did I use strong reasons?

❑  Did I treat each reason
separately?

❑  Did I support each reason with
facts and examples?

❑  Did I clearly state my goal?

## Questions for a Writing Conference

• What do you like about this piece?

• Are the opinion and the goal clear?

• Will the reasons convince the audience?
If not, why?

• Have possible objections been
addressed?

• Are any parts unclear?

Write notes to remember ideas discussed in your writing conference.

## My Notes

_____

_____

_____

_____

_____

_____

_____

_____

_____

_____

# Let the Falcon Fly!

Complete each sentence with a word from the box. Then cut out
the falcon and its cage. Fold up the sides of the cage so the
sentences are on the outside. Put the falcon in the cage and close
the top of the cage. After you read each sentence on the outside
of the cage, open that side of the cage. When you've read all four
sentences, you'll have set the falcon free!

> endure
> captivity
> liberty
> warily
> clashed

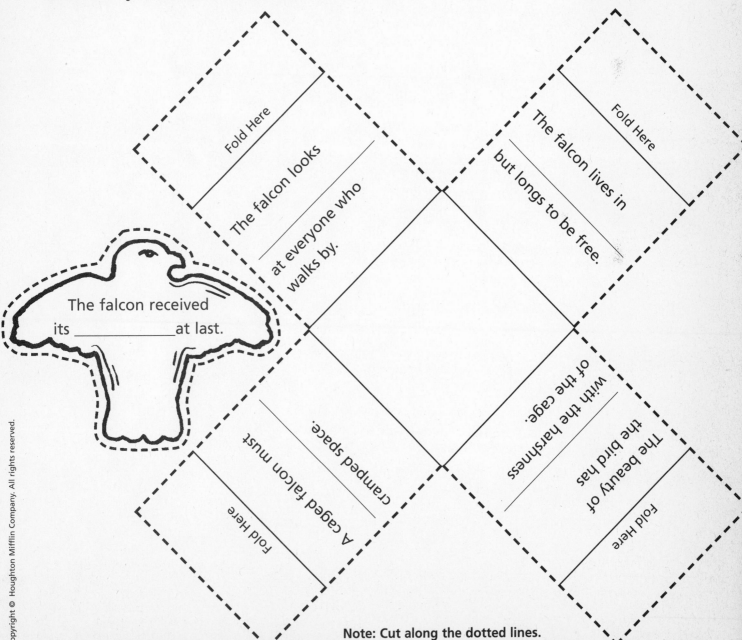

The falcon looks _____ at everyone who walks by.

The falcon lives in _____ but longs to be free.

The falcon received its _____ at last.

A caged falcon must _____ cramped space.

The beauty of the bird has _____ with the harshness of the cage.

**Note: Cut along the dotted lines.**

Name _____

# From Captivity to Freedom

The pictures show events from *Adiós falcón/Good-bye, Falcon*. Write a caption that tells what event the picture illustrates.

**1** _____

_____

_____

**2** _____

_____

_____

**3** _____

_____

_____

**4** _____

_____

_____

**5** _____

_____

_____

Name

# Take Your Ideas and Fly

**Read the pages referred to in the eggs. Then write your answers on the lines.**

1. Read the paragraph on page 190 that begins, "Duranté todo . . ." or page 191 that begins, "For the rest . . ." What is the main idea?

2. Read pages 192–193. What main ideas did you notice on these pages?

3. Read pages 194–195. What details support the main idea that the falcon is frightened to be let out of the cage?

**1** _____

_____

_____

**2** _____

_____

_____

**3** _____

_____

_____

**What was the topic of _Adiós falcón/Good-bye, Falcon_?**

_____

**Write a summary of the selection on a separate sheet of paper. Use the answers you gave above to help you.**

Name

# The Wild Life

Imagine that you are the editor of a wildlife magazine.
A writer has given you the following article, but you
only have space for five sentences. Combine the ten
sentences in the article into five.

Falconry has existed for over three thousand years. Falconry was an ancient Chinese and Persian sport. A falconer is a unique kind of hunter. A falconer uses falcons to hunt game. Falconers often use the peregrine falcon because it can dive after its victims at speeds close to two hundred miles per hour! The peregrine is a very fast bird of prey.

I spoke yesterday with Robert Vivez about training falcons. Mr. Vivez is a falcon owner and trainer. He explained that an eyas can be easily trained. A young falcon that has not learned to fly is called an eyas.

**1** _____

_____

_____

**2** _____

_____

_____

**3** _____

_____

_____

**4** _____

_____

_____

**5** _____

_____

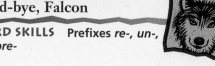

.............................................
Name

# Free as a Bird

**Read this diary page. Underline each word with a prefix and circle the prefix.**

| Prefix | Meaning |
|--------|---------|
| re- | again, back |
| un- | not, the opposite of |
| pre- | before, in advance |

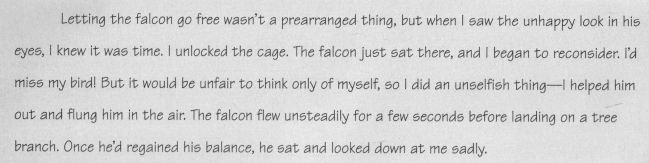

Letting the falcon go free wasn't a prearranged thing, but when I saw the unhappy look in his eyes, I knew it was time. I unlocked the cage. The falcon just sat there, and I began to reconsider. I'd miss my bird! But it would be unfair to think only of myself, so I did an unselfish thing—I helped him out and flung him in the air. The falcon flew unsteadily for a few seconds before landing on a tree branch. Once he'd regained his balance, he sat and looked down at me sadly.

Now it's nighttime, and I'm worried. My bird might be afraid and could even be in danger! Maybe I should have let him reenter his cage just for the first night, as a precaution. I hope he's okay!

**Now write the words you underlined. Use the chart to write the meaning of each word.**

**1** _____

**2** _____

**3** _____

**4** _____

**5** _____

**6** _____

**7** _____

**8** _____

**9** _____

**10** _____

# Captive in a Cage

Complete each phrase in the word web with a word from the box.

| clashed | endure | captivity | warily | liberty |
|---------|--------|-----------|--------|---------|
| captured | cautiously | escape | liberate | captive |

lives in
_____
but longs to be free

looks
_____
and _____
at everyone who
walks by

must
_____
a cramped space

longs for
_____

immediately
thought the cage
_____ with
the wide open skies

If the falcon in the story could talk, what would he say? Use the rest of the words in the box to write a paragraph that describes how the bird wins his freedom.

_____

_____

_____

_____

Name

# Falcon Flight

**Vowel + *r* Sounds in *bird*** Each Spelling
Word has the vowel + *r* sounds, shown as |ûr|, that
you hear in *bird*. The |ûr| sounds are often spelled
with the patterns *er*, *ir*, *ur*, *ear*, and *or*.

|ûr|   perch   bird   return   learn   world

**Write each Spelling Word under the matching
spelling pattern for the |ûr| sounds.**

## Spelling Words

1. bird
2. perch
3. return
4. learn
5. hurt
6. world
7. prefer
8. firm
9. worth
10. early

### My Study List
What other words do you
need to study for spelling?
Add them to My Study List for *Adiós
falcón/Good-bye, Falcon* in the back
of this book.

|ûr|   **er**

1 _____

2 _____

|ûr|   **ir**

3 _____

4 _____

|ûr|   **ur**

5 _____

6 _____

|ûr|   **ear**

7 _____

8 _____

|ûr|   **or**

9 _____

10 _____

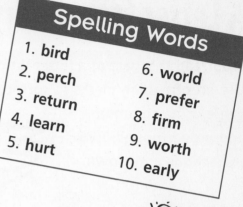

# Spelling Spree

**Proofreading** Find and circle six misspelled
Spelling Words in this student's report. Then write
each word correctly.

## Spelling Words

1. bird
2. perch
3. return
4. learn
5. hurt
6. world
7. prefer
8. firm
9. worth
10. early

A falcon is a byrd of prey. Falcons
purch their nests on steep cliffs. Their
babies learn to fly and hunt at an erly age.

Once falcons could be found in many
parts of the werlt, but later too many
pesticides were used. They hirt the falcon
eggs. The shells became less furm, so the
eggs broke very easily. Falcons are much
rarer now.

① _____     ③ _____     ⑤ _____

② _____     ④ _____     ⑥ _____

**Goof Proof** Professor Zoof often gets mixed up. Write a Spelling
Word that means the opposite of each underlined word in his speech.

7. People can <u>teach</u> about nature by watching falcons.

8. Falcons <u>dislike</u> uncrowded areas with clean water and air.

9. We will not <u>go</u> to a place where food is hard to find.

10. The lessons falcons teach people show the <u>uselessness</u> of
birdwatching!!

⑦ _____     ⑨ _____

⑧ _____     ⑩ _____

 **View of the Wild** You cannot always study a real animal in the
wild, but you can learn about it from a TV show. What would you
want to see during a program on your favorite wild animal? On a
separate sheet of paper, make a list of sentences that tell what
details to include in the TV show. Use Spelling Words from the list.

Name

# A Letter from Puerto Rico

**Proofread this part of a letter written by a visitor to Puerto Rico.
Use proofreading marks to correct the mistakes the writer
made using common
and proper nouns. Two
corrections are shown.**

Nouns

**Common**
girl
park
store

**Proper**
Anita
Central Park
Joe's Market

## Proofreading Marks

/ **Make a letter small.**
≡ **Make a capital letter.**

14 Calle marina

Playa Øe Ponce, Puerto Rico 00731

january 15, 1996

Dear andre,

Hello from an Island in the Caribbean sea! San juan, the Capital, is very

interesting. On monday aunt Clara took the family to the beach and

brought burritos and Bananas for lunch. The surf was great!

Unfortunately, my Uncle could not come.

**Now write each noun in the letter correctly in the chart.**

| Common Nouns | | Proper Nouns | |
|---|---|---|---|
| | | | |
| | | | |
| | | | |
| | | | |
| | | | |

# A Bird World

On a separate sheet of paper, create a tourist map for a bird refuge.
Cut out each picture and glue it on your map to show where to find
that item. Label each picture with a proper noun. Then complete the
map key by writing a common noun to label each picture. Cut out the
key and glue it to your map.

**Example:** Woodland
Trail

hiking
trail

Draw pictures for two ideas of your own.

Write a name for your refuge. Then write a brief
description of the refuge to interest tourists.
Attach it to your map.

## Map Key

**In the Wild** 79

Name

# Letter to the Editor

Write a Letter to the Editor that convinces readers of the importance of protecting a specific wild animal. Think of the ways humans affect this creature, such as by hunting or using pesticides. What points do you want to emphasize? How can readers change their behavior in order to protect this animal?

Your letter should have two or three main ideas that give your opinion of why it's important to protect this animal. Include factual details to support each main idea. Complete the chart to help you plan your letter.

Animal: _____

| Main Ideas (Opinions) | Supporting Details (Facts) | |
|---|---|---|
| 1. | a. | |
| | b. | |
| | c. | |
| 2. | a. | |
| | b. | |
| | c. | |
| 3. | a. | |
| | b. | |
| | c. | |

Your Letter to the Editor should show that you understand some ways in which human beings are responsible for the survival of the natural world. Use this checklist to check your work.

## Checklist

☐ My letter tells readers how to protect the animal I have described.

☐ Each paragraph has one main idea and supporting details.

☐ I back up all my opinions with facts.

Name

# Try to See It My Way

How do the characters in the stories see things in a new way? After reading each selection, answer the questions to complete the chart.

| | In the Year of the Boar and Jackie Robinson | Like Jake and Me |
|---|---|---|
| Who are the main characters? | | |
| What problems do the main characters have? | | |
| What does one character discover about another character? | | |
| What does a character learn or understand through another character or characters? | | |

Name

# Try to See It My Way

How do the characters in the stories see things in a new way? After
reading each selection, answer the questions to complete the chart.

| | Me, Mop, and the Moondance Kid | Felita |
|---|---|---|
| **Who are the main characters?** | | |
| **What problems do the main characters have?** | | |
| **What does one character discover about another character?** | | |
| **What does a character learn or understand through another character or characters?** | | |

What have you learned in this theme about there being
more than one point of view to every story?

_____

_____

# Dear Diary

**Use each word from the box to complete the sentences. Then answer the questions.**

| foreign | foreigner | ambassador |
|---------|-----------|------------|
| reputation | escapade | |

**Monday**

I've been in the United States for two days now. The food seems so

_____ to me! Sometimes it's hard being a

_____ in a new country. Mother told me that I am an

_____ for the Chinese people. If I behave well, we will all

have a good _____.

**Tuesday**

My new friend and I were baby-sitting his little sister when all of a sudden she was

gone! We were worried and looked all around the apartment for her. Finally, we found

her sleeping behind the couch. What an _____!

**1** What is an escapade a person could have?

_____

**2** What could a person do to get a good reputation?

_____

**3** What language would be foreign to you?

_____

**4** What question would you ask an ambassador?

_____

**5** What question might a foreigner ask you?

_____

Name

# Shirley's Eventful Day

**Answer the questions about Shirley's first day of school.**

What mistake does the principal make when she enrolls Shirley?

What strange foreign custom does Shirley learn about from watching the principal?

What adventure does Shirley have at lunchtime?

Why is Shirley worried when she comes back to her class?

Why does Mrs. Rappaport write that she thinks there is something wrong with Shirley's eyes?

Name

# Details, Details!

**Think about all of Shirley's new experiences.**
**Then answer the questions.**

What are some details
Shirley notices . . .

What are some details you
notice about Shirley . . .

. . . about the principal?

. . . that show she is worried
when she returns to her
classroom after lunch?

. . . about her classmates?

. . . that show Shirley is afraid
to give the letter to her
parents?

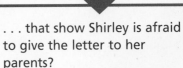 Try to See It My Way 87

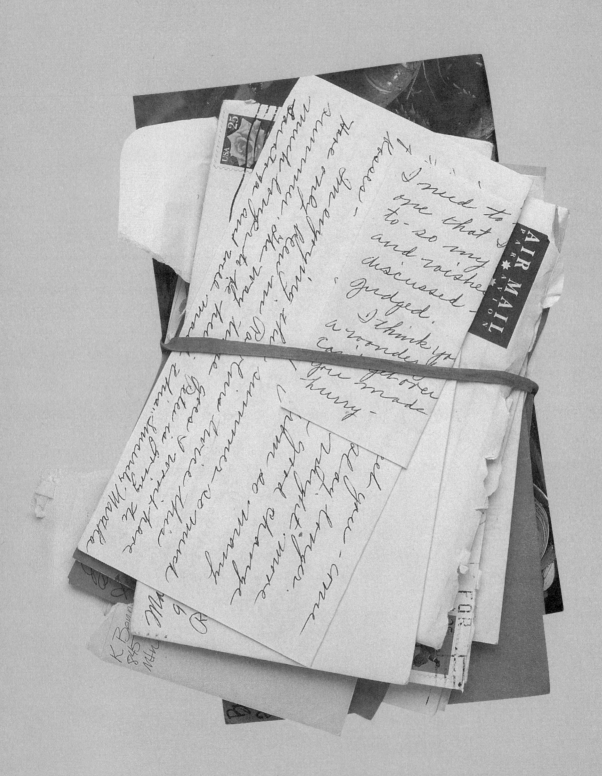

Name _____

# From Me to You

The envelope for a letter should include the name and address
of the person receiving the letter and the name and address of
the person sending the letter.

> **Return Address** (sender's name and address)
> name
> street address/apartment
> town, state   Zip Code

Susan Johnson
515 Highland Ave.
Brooklyn, NY 11224

> **Address**
> name
> street address/apartment
> town, state   Zip Code

Miss Shirley Temple Wong
481 Main St., Apt. A
Brooklyn, NY 11201

**In the center of the address label, write the name and address of
someone you write to. Write your return address in the upper left
corner of the label. Cut out the label and use it on your letter.**

Name _____

# Winking and Blinking

On Shirley's first day at an American school, her teacher thought there
was something wrong with her eyes. Solve the puzzle to find out why
Shirley kept blinking at people.

Write the base word or suffix of each word. Then write each numbered
letter on the line with the matching number at the bottom of the page.

**1** suffix of *retirement*     ___ ___ ___ ___
                                       12

**2** base word of *correction*  ___ ___ ___ ___ ___ ___
                                      6   9

**3** suffix of *courtship*      ___ ___ ___ ___
                                  2       17

**4** base word of *festivity*   ___ ___ ___ ___ ___ ___
                                  8      14      3

**5** suffix of *scarcity*       ___ ___ ___
                                  10

**6** base word of *judgment*    ___ ___ ___ ___
                                          13  4

**7** suffix of *election*       ___ ___ ___
                                          5

**8** base word of *fellowship*  ___ ___ ___ ___ ___ ___
                                  7   11

**9** suffix of *oddity*         ___ ___ ___
                                  16

**10** base word of *achievement* ___ ___ ___ ___ ___ ___
                                   1       15

Shirley thought that blinking was

___ ___ ___ ___ ___   ___ ___
 1   2   3   4   5     6   7

___ ___ ___ ___ ___ ___ ___ ___ ___ ___ .
 8   9   10  11  12  13  14  15  16  17

Try to See It My Way   91

Name

# Diplomatically Speaking

Match the words to their definitions. Write
one letter of the word in each blank. Then use
the numbered letters to solve the puzzle.

| honor | daring |
| exploit | foreign |
| embassy | diplomat |
| foreigner | escapade |
| reputation | ambassador |

**1** the headquarters of an official
who represents his or her country

\_\_ \_\_ \_\_ \_\_ \_\_ \_\_ \_\_
$\quad\quad\quad$ 10 $\quad\quad\quad$ 3

**2** what the public thinks of a
person

\_\_ \_\_ \_\_ \_\_ \_\_ \_\_ \_\_ \_\_ \_\_ \_\_
$\quad\quad\quad$ 7 $\quad\quad\quad\quad\quad\quad$ 13

**3** a person from another country

\_\_ \_\_ \_\_ \_\_ \_\_ \_\_ \_\_ \_\_
$\quad$ 6

**4** a heroic act

\_\_ \_\_ \_\_ \_\_ \_\_ \_\_ \_\_
$\quad\quad\quad\quad$ 12

**5** a high-ranking official who
represents his or her country

\_\_ \_\_ \_\_ \_\_ \_\_ \_\_ \_\_ \_\_ \_\_ \_\_
$\quad\quad\quad\quad$ 11 $\quad\quad\quad\quad\quad$ 2

**6** someone who is skilled at
international relations

\_\_ \_\_ \_\_ \_\_ \_\_ \_\_ \_\_ \_\_
8 $\quad\quad$ 5

**7** respect

\_\_ \_\_ \_\_ \_\_ \_\_
9

**8** willing to take risks

\_\_ \_\_ \_\_ \_\_ \_\_ \_\_
$\quad\quad\quad\quad$ 14

**9** from another country

\_\_ \_\_ \_\_ \_\_ \_\_ \_\_ \_\_
$\quad\quad\quad$ 1

**10** an adventure

\_\_ \_\_ \_\_ \_\_ \_\_ \_\_ \_\_ \_\_
$\quad$ 4

Shirley was sad to leave her home in China. However, once
she made some new friends in America, she realized that the
following saying was true.

\_\_ V \_\_ \_\_ \_\_ $\quad$ \_\_ \_\_ \_\_ \_\_ \_\_ $\quad$ \_\_ \_\_ \_\_
1 $\quad$ 1 $\quad$ 2 $\quad$ 3 $\quad\quad$ 4 $\quad$ 5 $\quad$ 6 $\quad$ 7 $\quad$ 8 $\quad\quad$ 9 $\quad$ 10 $\quad$ 11

\_\_ $\quad$ \_\_ \_\_ \_\_ V \_\_ $\quad$ \_\_ \_\_ $\quad$ \_\_ \_\_ \_\_ \_\_ \_\_ .
10 $\quad$ 11 $\quad$ 12 $\quad$ 5 $\quad\quad$ 1 $\quad$ 2 $\quad\quad$ 5 $\quad$ 12 $\quad$ 13 $\quad$ 12 $\quad$ 13 $\quad$ 14

# Dog or Dragon

## The Vowel Sounds in *shout* and *wall*

Some Spelling Words have the |ou| sound that you hear in *shout.* The |ou| sound is usually spelled with the pattern *ou* or *ow*.

|ou|    shout   allow

The other Spelling Words have the |ô| sound that you hear in *dawn.* The |ô| sound is usually spelled with the pattern *aw*, *au*, or *a* before *l*.

|ô|    dawn   fault   wall

### Spelling Words

1. shout
2. wall
3. allow
4. counter
5. although
6. fault
7. frown
8. pause
9. dawn
10. straw

### My Study List
What other words do you need to study for spelling? Add them to My Study List for *In the Year of the Boar and Jackie Robinson* in the back of this book.

Shirley's story takes place during the Chinese Year of the Boar. Write each Spelling Word under the sign for the Chinese Year with the matching sound and spelling pattern.

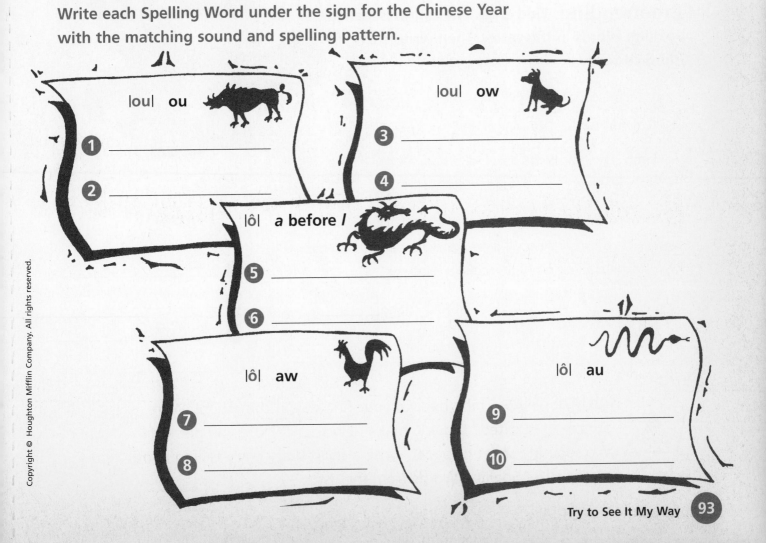

|ou|  **ou**

1. _____

2. _____

|ou|  **ow**

3. _____

4. _____

|ô|  *a before l*

5. _____

6. _____

|ô|  **aw**

7. _____

8. _____

|ô|  **au**

9. _____

10. _____

................................................

Name

# Spelling Spree

## The Third Word   Write the Spelling Word that belongs in each group of words.

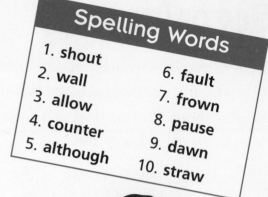

**Spelling Words**

1. shout
2. wall
3. allow
4. counter
5. although
6. fault
7. frown
8. pause
9. dawn
10. straw

**1** floor, ceiling, _____

**2** cupboard, shelf, _____

**3** stop, start, _____

**4** wheat, hay, _____

**5** talk, whisper, _____

**6** blame, mistake, _____

## Proofreading   Find and circle four misspelled Spelling Words in this letter. Then write each word correctly.

Dear Mai Mai,

   Each day I awake at daun, and I pause to think of you. I wonder what you are doing today!

   My new school is very different, altho I like it. My teacher is so nice. She will alow me extra time to do my work and does not froun if I make a mistake.

                     Your friend,
                     Shirley

**7** _____

**8** _____

**9** _____

**10** _____

## School Days   Think back to your first day in this school. Were you scared? Excited? Did you make new friends? Did you get lost? On a separate sheet of paper, write a short diary entry telling about your day. Use Spelling Words from the list.

Name ......................................................

# Lunch with Mr. P

**Adjectives** Mr. P wants to attract more customers to his store.
Help him write an advertisement by adding adjectives.

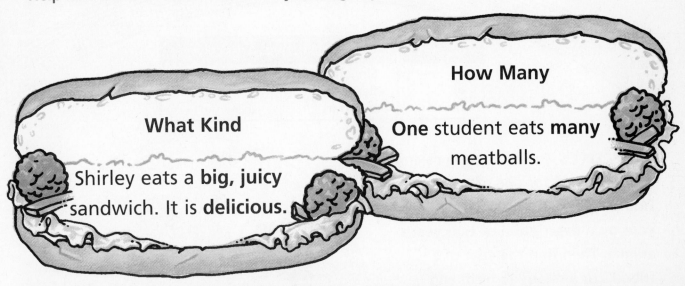

**What Kind**

Shirley eats a **big, juicy** sandwich. It is **delicious.**

**How Many**

**One** student eats **many** meatballs.

## Pick Mr. P's

Mr. P's tasty treats will make your mouth water! You can buy

_____ frozen yogurt or _____ pizza.
　　(what kind)　　　　　　　　　　　　　　　　　　　　(what kind)

How would you like _____ _____
　　　　　　　　　　　　　(how many)　　　　　　　　　(what kind)

peanuts and a _____ juice? Tired of candy? Mr. P has
　　　　　　　　　　(what kind)

_____ fruit to refresh your mouth.  Be sure to have
　　(what kind)

_____ pieces! And don't forget _____
　　(how many)　　　　　　　　　　　　　　　　　　　　(what kind)

popcorn. Just _____ bag will fill you right up. There are
　　　　　　　　　　(how many)

_____ treats we haven't even mentioned.
　　(how many)

Come to Mr. P's and try them all!

Name _____

# In the Year of the __?__

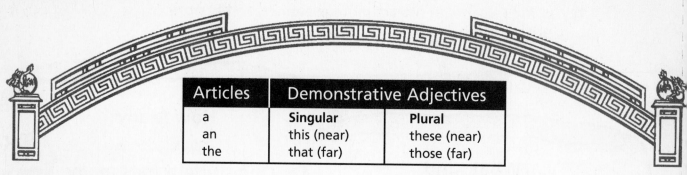

| Articles | Demonstrative Adjectives | |
|----------|--------------------------|--|
| | **Singular** | **Plural** |
| a | this (near) | these (near) |
| an | | |
| the | that (far) | those (far) |

**Adjectives** In the Chinese calendar, each year is named for one of twelve animals. Find the year you were born and write your own description of that year's animal. Then find the year of a friend's or a relative's birth and write a description of that animal. Underline articles, demonstrative adjectives, and descriptive adjectives.

**Birth year** _____ **Animal** _____

**Birth year** _____ **Animal** _____

Name

# Painting with Words

### Ideas for Description Topics

- the school bus
- the bus driver
- the lady on the train
- my secret hangout
- lunchtime at school

- my homemade pizza
- the scene from my classroom window
- my favorite shoes
- my baseball bat
- my grandfather

## My Description Topics

**List five people, places, things, or events that you know well enough to describe.**

_____

_____

_____

_____

_____

**Think about each idea you wrote.**
**Ask yourself these questions.**

*Have I seen this person, place, thing, or event recently?*

*Can I use at least three senses to describe it?*

*Would I enjoy writing about it?*

**Circle the topic you want to write about.**

Name _____

# Use Your Senses

Complete the cluster with descriptive details about how your topic looks, sounds, tastes, smells, or feels to the touch. Write exact words or descriptive phrases that you might want to use.

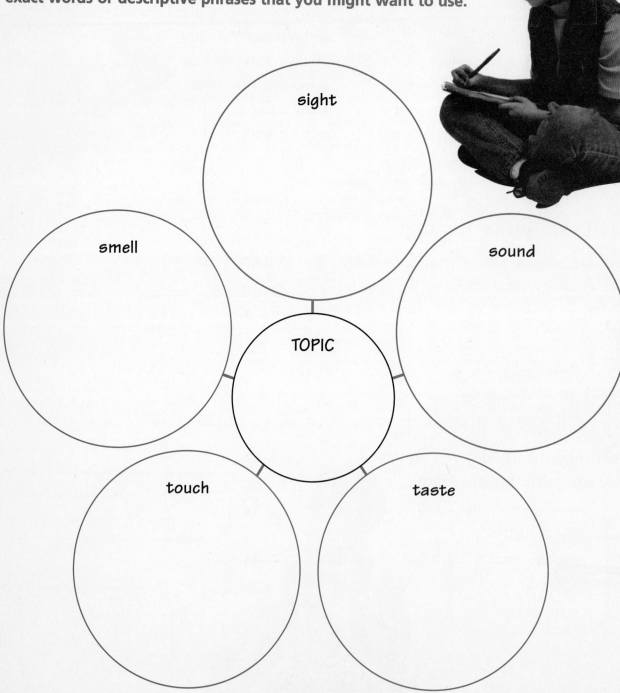

sight

smell

sound

TOPIC

touch

taste

Name

# Taking a Fresh Look

Reread and revise your description, using the Revising Checklist.
Then use the Questions for a Writing Conference to help you
discuss your questions with a partner.

## Revising Checklist

☐ Did I focus on describing my topic rather then telling about a personal experience?

☐ Did I use details that appeal to different senses?

☐ Did I use descriptive language, such as exact words, similes, and metaphors?

☐ Are the details organized in a way that is easy to follow?

## Questions for a Writing Conference

• What is good about this description?

• What details are given? What other details would help fill out the picture?

• Are there any details that do not belong?

• Which general words could be replaced with exact words?

• What similes or metaphors are used? Are they helpful? Where could others be used?

Write notes to remember ideas and comments from your writing conference.

## My Notes

_____

_____

_____

_____

_____

_____

_____

_____

Name _____

# Ready for Action

Read each sentence. After each sentence, write the word from the box that means the same as the underlined phrase.

| gasped | grappled | swaggered | crouched | thundered |
|--------|----------|-----------|----------|-----------|

**1** Alex lowered himself to the ground and waited. _____

**2** When Jake walked by, Alex jumped up and moved with a loud booming noise past him. _____

**3** Alex grabbed and struggled with the doorknob of the front door.

_____

**4** Jake drew in breath sharply as he ran after Alex. _____

**5** Alex moved proudly into the house and announced, "I beat Jake!"

_____

Answer each question.

**6** Have you ever gasped at something? Why?

_____

**7** Write about something that thundered when it moved. Why did it make a lot of noise?

_____

**8** Have you ever crouched in order to do something? Tell what it was.

_____

**9** Did you ever help someone who grappled with something? Tell how.

_____

**10** Have you ever swaggered because of something you did? Tell what it was.

_____

Name _____

# Spider Web

**Read the quotes from *Like Jake and Me*, and then add the missing information.**

"Do . . . you . . . need . . . me . . . to . . . help?"

Who says?_____

To whom?_____

Why?_____

_____

"Jake isn't the ballet type."

Who says?_____

To whom?_____

Why?_____

_____

"Maybe like Jake *and* you."

Who says?_____

To whom?_____

Why?_____

"Wolf spider! Where?"

Who says?_____

To whom?_____

Why?_____

_____

"May I have this dance?"

Who says?_____

To whom?_____

Why?_____

_____

# Compare the Pair

Think of at least four ways that Virginia and the wolf spider are alike and four ways they are different. Then complete the Venn diagram to compare and contrast Virginia and the wolf spider.

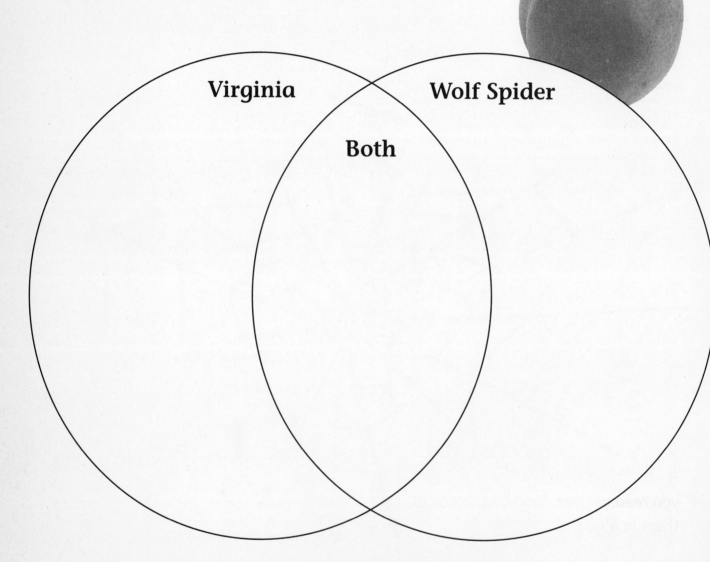

Virginia        Wolf Spider

Both

Now write a sentence comparing Virginia and the wolf spider.

_____

_____

_____

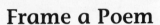

Name

# Poem Prompters

Having trouble writing a poem? Try one or more of these activities to spark ideas.

## Frame a Poem

Create a frame for your topic that you can use for each line or to begin different sections.

**Examples:** If wishes came true . . .

Red is . . .

My mother says . . .

At night . . .

Write some frames for your own ideas.

## Be an Observer

Observe people. What are they feeling or thinking?

Observe things. What do they mean to you or remind you of?

Carry a notebook and write down your observations for a day. Can you find a poem in them?

## Draw a Poem

Draw a picture of something important to you. Write your thoughts and feelings about it. Can you write a poem about it?

## Cool Words

Poetic language is all around you—just keep your eyes and ears open. Write down interesting words and phrases that you read or hear. Can you use any of them in a poem?

Name

# Hide and Seek

The wolf spider was as scared of Jake as he was of her. Solve the puzzle to find out where she hid. Use words from the box to fill in the blanks. Then unscramble the letters in the circles to spell the wolf spider's hiding place.

| light | always | smart | trash | destroy | unhappy | mistake | after |

**1** an antonym for **heavy** __ __ __ ◯ __

**2** a synonym for **sad** __ __ __ ◯ __ __

**3** a synonym for **ruin** __ ◯ __ __ __ __ __

**4** an antonym for **before** __ ◯ __ __ __

**5** a synonym for **garbage** ◯ __ __ __ __

**6** an antonym for **stupid** __ __ __ ◯ __

**7** an antonym for **never** ◯ __ __ __ __ __

**8** a synonym for **error** __ __ __ __ __ __ ◯

The wolf spider's hiding place:

__ __ __ __ __ __

Name

# Spider Synonyms

Each wolf spider is next to a definition. Each definition matches two synonyms. Cut out the synonyms and paste them next to the correct definition. Then write a sentence using one of the synonyms.

walked proudly

_____

_____

struggled

_____

_____

bent down low

_____

_____

spoke while out
of breath

_____

_____

made loud sounds

_____

_____

| | |
|---|---|
| | grappled |
| | panted |
| | thundered |
| | wrestled |
| | gasped |
| | crouched |
| | strutted |
| | squatted |
| | boomed |
| | swaggered |

# Word Spiders

**Final Schwa + *r* Sounds**  Each Spelling Word has more than one syllable and ends with the schwa sound + *r*, shown as |ər|. The schwa sound, shown as |ə|, is a weak vowel sound that is often found in an unstressed syllable. The final |ər| sounds in words of more than one syllable are often spelled with the pattern *er*, *or*, or *ar*.

|ər|    spid**er**    col**or**    coll**ar**

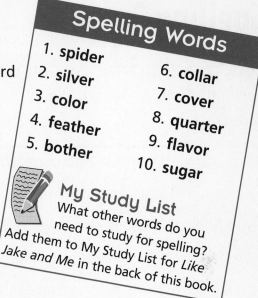

## Spelling Words

1. spider
2. silver
3. color
4. feather
5. bother
6. collar
7. cover
8. quarter
9. flavor
10. sugar

**My Study List**
What other words do you need to study for spelling? Add them to My Study List for *Like Jake and Me* in the back of this book.

Write the missing pattern to complete each Spelling Word around the spider. Then write each word under the correct spelling pattern.

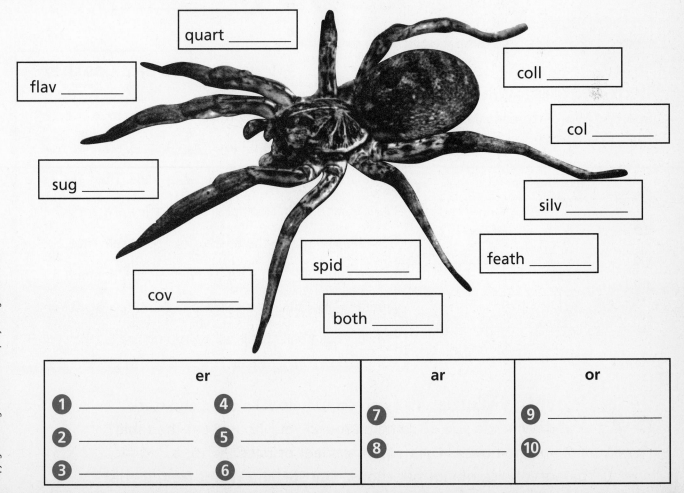

quart _____

flav _____

coll _____

col _____

sug _____

silv _____

cov _____

spid _____

both _____

feath _____

| er | | ar | or |
|---|---|---|---|
| 1 _____ | 4 _____ | 7 _____ | 9 _____ |
| 2 _____ | 5 _____ | 8 _____ | 10 _____ |
| 3 _____ | 6 _____ | | |

Name

# Spelling Spree

**Proofreading**  Find and circle five misspelled
Spelling Words in this ad. Then write each word
correctly.

Surprise someone you love
with one of these charming
silver pins! Choose the cowboy hat with
its tiny fether. Or order the spidar with its
glittery eyes the coler of emeralds. Each is
about the size of a quater and will look
great on a shirt coller or
pocket. Buy both and save!

1 _____
2 _____
3 _____
4 _____
5 _____

**Pear Leather**  Write
Spelling Words to complete
this recipe.

6 _____
7 _____
8 _____
9 _____
10 _____

### Pear Leather

Cut pears in chunks, but don't _____ to peel or core
them. Put pears in a large _____ kettle. (Do not use
aluminum.) Add one cup water or juice. Then _____ the
kettle with a lid. Cook pears until they are soft.
Strain and mash the pears. Sweeten them with one or
more cups of _____; also add ginger or cinnamon for
more _____. Put in a shallow pan and bake at 300° F
for several hours until fairly dry and like leather.

**Warning Words**  Alex wanted to help Jake chop and stack
wood. What do you do to help around your house? Set the table?
Take out the trash? On a separate sheet of paper, write a
paragraph describing your chores. Use Spelling Words from the list.

# Knee Slappers

| | |
|---|---|
| hairy | cheerful |
| hairier than #1 | more cheerful than #1 |
| hairiest of all | most cheerful of all |

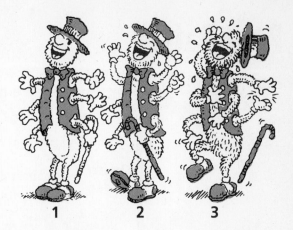

1    2    3

**Comparing with Adjectives** Here are
some jokes Alex might try out on Jake.
Complete each joke by writing the correct form of the adjective.
Then write your own joke, using an adjective in a comparison.

**1** Why is heat (fast) _____ than cold?

**2** Why is bowling the (quiet) _____ sport of all?

**3** Why is basketball the (disgusting) _____ sport?

**4** Which is (generous) _____, a giraffe or a skunk?

**5** What is the (easy) _____ way to clean a tuba?

**6** What are the (big) _____ bugs in the world?

**7** Which dinosaur is (scary) _____ than a velociraptor?

**8** Why are smiles (long) _____ than frowns?

**9** Who is the (nosy) _____ superhero of all?

**10** Who is the (well-traveled) _____ superhero of all?

**Answers:**

1. You can catch cold.
2. You can hear a pin drop.
3. The players dribble all over the court.
4. A skunk: it gives everyone around it a scent.
5. With a tuba toothpaste.
6. Gi-ants
7. A terror-dactyl
8. There's a mile between the beginning and the end.
9. Snooperman
10. Wander Woman

**My Joke:** _____

_____

# Pear Patter

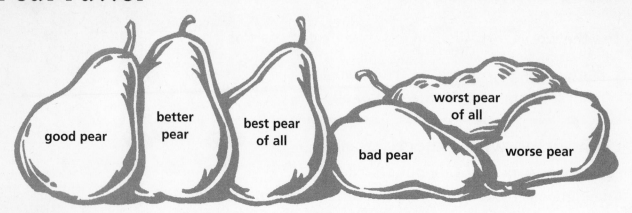

good pear

better
pear

best pear
of all

worst pear
of all

bad pear

worse pear

**Comparing with Adjectives** Virginia wants to sell jars of her pear
preserves. She has tried to write a commercial for the local radio station,
but she is not sure how she should use *good* and *bad* in comparisons.
Help complete Virginia's commercial. Give her pear preserves a name,
cross out each misuse of *good* or *bad*, and write the correct form over it.
Add your own ending, using a comparison with *good* or *bad*.

Commercial for _____
(name of product)

Want a sweet treat? Candy can be the baddest snack of all. In fact, few things

are badder  for you than candy. Instead, try _____.

Made with the freshest, goodest  pears, it is naturally delicious. Spread it on

bread, or, for the goodest  treat of all, eat it right out of the jar. But be careful.

Every taste gets gooder  and gooder,  so you might eat the whole jar. Things

could be badder,  though. Just buy more!

Virginia: Try this ending.

_____

_____

_____

_____

Name

# Batter Up

Use the words from the box to complete each part of
the announcer's report. Then answer the question.

| series | squad |
| backstop | foul |

It's the Lions against the Lambs.

The _____

is tied at two games each. The

score is 12 to 12 in the last inning.

The Lions are up at bat. The batter

swings . . . and it's a

_____ ball.

It's amazing! The Lambs' first baseman has

thrown the ball all the way to the _____

and now it's bouncing back onto the field!

Four runs! The Lions win with a roar! We have

our new champions, the best _____

in the country, the Lions!

**What do you think it
would be like to be in
the play-offs?**

_____
_____
_____
_____

# Baseball Ups and Downs

Answer each question.

1 Why is winning the game important for the Elks?

_____

_____

_____

_____

2 How does T.J. feel when he misses the ball? How do you know?

_____

_____

_____

4 What are T.J.'s and Moondance's problems?

_____

_____

_____

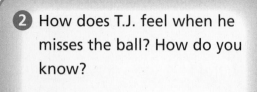

3 Why do Marla, Mr. Williams, and Sister Carmelita help Moondance with his pitching?

_____

_____

_____

Name

# See It Both Ways: You Make the Calls!

Will the Elks make it to the play-offs? Complete each chart
with three story events and two examples from your own
experiences that support the predicted outcome.

## WINNERS

| EVENTS | EXPERIENCES | PREDICTED OUTCOME |
|---|---|---|
| 1. | 1. | The Elks will make the play-offs. |
| 2. | 2. | |
| 3. | | |

## LOSERS

| EVENTS | EXPERIENCES | PREDICTED OUTCOME |
|---|---|---|
| 1. | 1. | The Elks won't make the play-offs. |
| 2. | 2. | |
| 3. | | |

Name

# Play Ball!

The sports editor wants to shorten this article to make room for photos. Rewrite the article, combining sentences to form new sentences with compound subjects or compound predicates. Use a separate sheet of paper if you need more space.

## Lions Maul Tigers!

by Sheila Madigan

Yesterday the Lions and the Tigers fought to go to the play-offs.

The Lions were up first. They played brilliantly! The first batter got on base. The second batter got on base. The third batter got on base! The bases were loaded. Carlos Garcia was up next. Carlos Garcia hit a home run! The Lions cheered loudly. Their fans cheered loudly.

The Tigers were in trouble. Their pitcher loaded the bases two more times. He walked five batters. He struck out no one. That was only the first inning!

The Tigers were able to score two runs in the bottom of the first. The coach felt hopeful. The players felt hopeful. Then their luck ran out. They did not score again for the rest of the game.

The Lions played much better than the Tigers. They won the game easily. The final score was 21–2, Lions. The players are looking forward to the play-offs. Their coaches are looking forward to the play-offs.

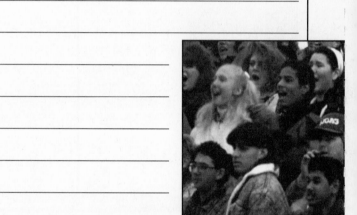

# Double Word Play

Solve each riddle by using a word from the box twice.
Each use of the word will have a different meaning.

| bleacher | pitcher | foul | bat | fan | fly | batter | ball |
|---|---|---|---|---|---|---|---|

**1** What would a baseball player who hits the ball make when he felt like having pancakes?

He'd make a

_____ _____

**2** What would you call a rotten way to hit a ball out of bounds?

It would be a

_____ _____

**3** What would you call a baseball player who throws water containers instead of baseballs?

She'd be a

_____ _____

**4** What wooden object would a small, black, winged mammal use to hit a baseball?

It would use a

_____ _____

**5** What would you call a small, black, flying insect that's hit straight up in the air?

It would be a

_____ _____

**6** What would you call an electric appliance that cools a person who is loyal to one baseball team?

You could call it a

_____ _____

**7** What would you call a person paid to turn the seats in the stadium white?

You could call him a

_____ _____

**8** What would you call a fancy dance for small, white, round objects?

It would be a

_____ _____

Name _____

# Team Picks

Each of the players has a word on his or her uniform. Write the correct player's
number on the line next to the definition that matches that player's word.

**1** a ball hit outside the playing area _____

**2** games played to determine a championship _____

**3** a group of consecutive games _____

**4** one of nine playing periods in a baseball game _____

**5** fence behind home plate that stops the ball from leaving the field _____

**6** position between second and third base _____

**7** threw the ball toward the batter _____

**8** a group of players on a team _____

**9** referee who stands behind the catcher _____

On a separate sheet of paper, write a paragraph using the players' words.

Name ....................................................

# Batting Practice

**Final Schwa + *l* Sounds**  Each Spelling Word
has two or more syllables and ends with the **schwa**
sound + ***l***, shown as ||əl|| or sometimes as only ||l||.
The final |əl| or |l| sounds are often spelled with
the pattern ***le***, ***el***, or ***al***.

|əl| or |l|    eag**le**    lev**el**    speci**al**

Be a power hitter!  Fill in the pattern that
spells the schwa + *l* sounds in each Spelling
Word in the ballpark.

**My Study List**
What other words do you
need to study for spelling?
Add them to My Study List for *Me,
Mop, and the Moondance Kid* in the
back of this book.

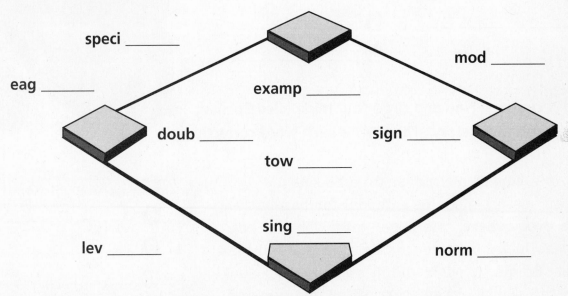

speci _____

mod _____

eag _____

examp _____

doub _____

sign _____

tow _____

sing _____

lev _____

norm _____

Now write each Spelling Word under the correct spelling pattern.

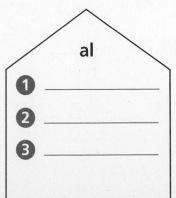

**al**

1 _____
2 _____
3 _____

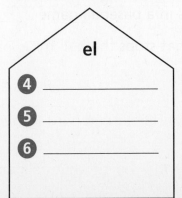

**el**

4 _____
5 _____
6 _____

**le**

7 _____
8 _____
9 _____
10 _____

Name _____

# Spelling Spree

## Tongue Twisters   Write a Spelling Word to complete each tongue twister.

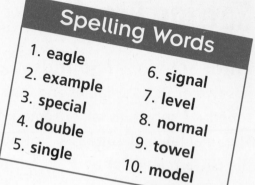
1. Steve slammed a _____ that sent Sam sliding to second.
2. Nina's nightly nightmares were not _____.
3. Leon's leaning lodge was not on _____ land.
4. Each eager _____ flew east easily.
5. Sue slowed to a stop as soon as she saw the _____.
6. Tammy tried to use Todd's T-shirt as a _____.

**1** _____        **4** _____

**2** _____        **5** _____

**3** _____        **6** _____

## Proofreading   Find and circle four misspelled Spelling Words in this news story.  Then write each word correctly.

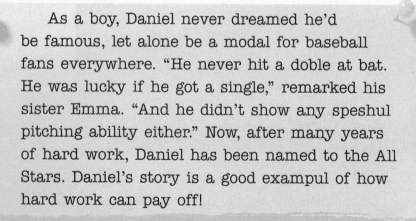

As a boy, Daniel never dreamed he'd be famous, let alone be a modal for baseball fans everywhere. "He never hit a doble at bat. He was lucky if he got a single," remarked his sister Emma. "And he didn't show any speshul pitching ability either." Now, after many years of hard work, Daniel has been named to the All Stars. Daniel's story is a good exampul of how hard work can pay off!

**7** _____

**8** _____

**9** _____

**10** _____

## Award Winner   Marla worked hard to teach T.J. and the team how to be good sports. On a separate sheet of paper, write a brief description of how a good sport should talk and act. Use Spelling Words from the list.

# Sports Extra!

action
verb        direct
object
The pitcher held the trophy.

**Action Verbs and Direct Objects**   Complete the news story, using words from the box. If the word is an action verb, circle the letter under **Action Verb**. If it is a direct object, circle the letter under **Direct Object**. Finally, write the circled letters in the blanks at the bottom of the page to find the answer to the riddle.

| heard | control | owned | it | earned | bat | bases | scored | won | name |
|---|---|---|---|---|---|---|---|---|---|

## Eagles Crush Pumas

The Eagles _____ the series easily today. The Pumas' first three batters loaded the _____. Then Abe Ruiz grabbed the _____, watched the ball, and swung. The fans _____ a loud crack, and the ball soared over the fence. Every player _____ a run. The crowd joyously screamed Abe's _____.

In the next inning, the Eagles took _____ and never lost _____. Tina Davis pitched and didn't give up a single run. At bat the Eagles _____ the ball, scoring and triumphing, 9–4. They _____ their trophy!

| | Action Verb | Direct Object |
|---|---|---|
| 1 | Y | M |
| 2 | S | O |
| 3 | E | U |
| 4 | R | N |
| 5 | B | I |
| 6 | L | R |
| 7 | I | E |
| 8 | C | A |
| 9 | T | P |
| 10 | H | K |

**Question:** What is harder to catch the faster you run?

**Answer:** __ __ __ __ __   __ __ __ __ __ __ __

Name _____

# Hot Headlines!

**Action Verbs and Direct Objects** Use one
action verb and one direct object to complete each of
these headlines from the sports pages of a newspaper.

**Example:** New Hockey Team <u>Breaks the Ice</u>

HOMETOWN HITTERS
_____
_____

Coach Buono
_____
_____

The Awesome Twosome
_____
_____

Undefeated Tadpoles
_____
_____

**Foul Ball**
_____
_____

**OLYMPIC STAR**
_____
_____

EXCITED FANS
_____
_____

**Donovan's Defeat**
_____
_____

**Sudden Rainstorm**
_____
_____

**HORNETS**
_____
_____

Name

# Puzzled?

Use each word from the box once to complete the puzzle about the play.

| casting | heroine | audition | recited | script | imitated |

**Down**

1. the choosing of the actors for the parts in a play
3. acted like someone else
6. one of the main characters in a play

**Across**

2. try out for a play
4. repeated words from memory
5. what you read when trying out for a play

Write a sentence using two words from the puzzle.

_____

_____

Name

# Scene by Scene

The writer forgot to complete the program for the play *Felita*. Think about what happened in each scene and complete the sentences.

## Felita

*Scene 1.*  At school just days before the audition,

_____

_____

_____

*Scene 2.*  At the audition for the part of Priscilla,

_____

_____

*Scene 3.*  On the morning of the play, in Felita's kitchen,

_____

_____

*Scene 4.*  At the cast party after the play,

_____

_____

*Scene 5.*  In Abuelita's apartment after dinner, Felita

_____

_____

*Scene 6.*  After school on Monday,

_____

# Deal With It!

How does each character solve one of her problems? Complete the chart and answer the questions.

| Character | Problem | Solution |
|-----------|---------|----------|
| Gigi | wants to be better than Felita at something | |
| Felita | | |

**1** Is Gigi's way of dealing with her problem a good one? Why or why not? _____

_____

**2** How else could Gigi have handled her problem? _____

_____

**3** Do you think Felita solved her problem in the best way possible? Explain your

answer. _____

_____

**4** Do you think Felita's and Gigi's problems could have been avoided? How?

_____

_____

......................................................................

Name

# What's Wrong?

Felita's brothers took messages for her when she was out, but something was wrong with each one. For each message, tell what important information was left out.

---

**MESSAGE 1**

Saturday, 1:00
Felita,
A friend called.
Can you go to the park tomorrow at noon?

---

**MESSAGE 2**

Saturday
Felita,
Miss Lovett called.
She has some questions about the art project.
She will call back in two hours.

---

**MESSAGE 3**

Saturday, 2:30
Felita,
Consuela called.
She said something about the art project; important.
She won't be home until tomorrow night; will call back.

---

| | What important information was left out? |
|---|---|
| **Message 1** | |
| **Message 2** | |
| **Message 3** | |

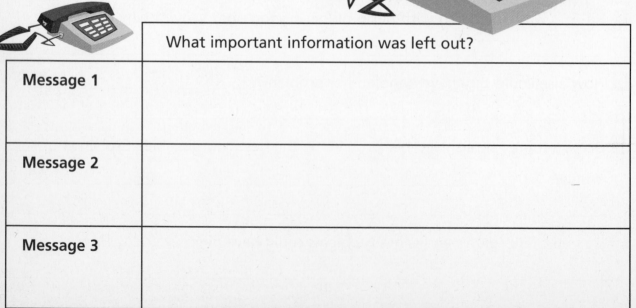

# Stage Fright

Nervous actors forgot some of their lines in the Thanksgiving play. The number of syllables in each forgotten word or phrase matches the number of the scene it's from. Write the word or phrase next to the correct scene.

harvested their crops

the brave military captain

sat for supper at a long table

a Thanksgiving Day feast

turkey, corn, and cranberries

the most beautiful maiden in Plymouth

ship

a new village

Pilgrims

Plymouth Rock

## Thanksgiving Play

### Act One

Scene 1: _____

Scene 2: _____

Scene 3: _____

Scene 4: _____

Scene 5: _____

Scene 6: _____

Scene 7: _____

Scene 8: _____

Scene 9: _____

Scene 10: _____

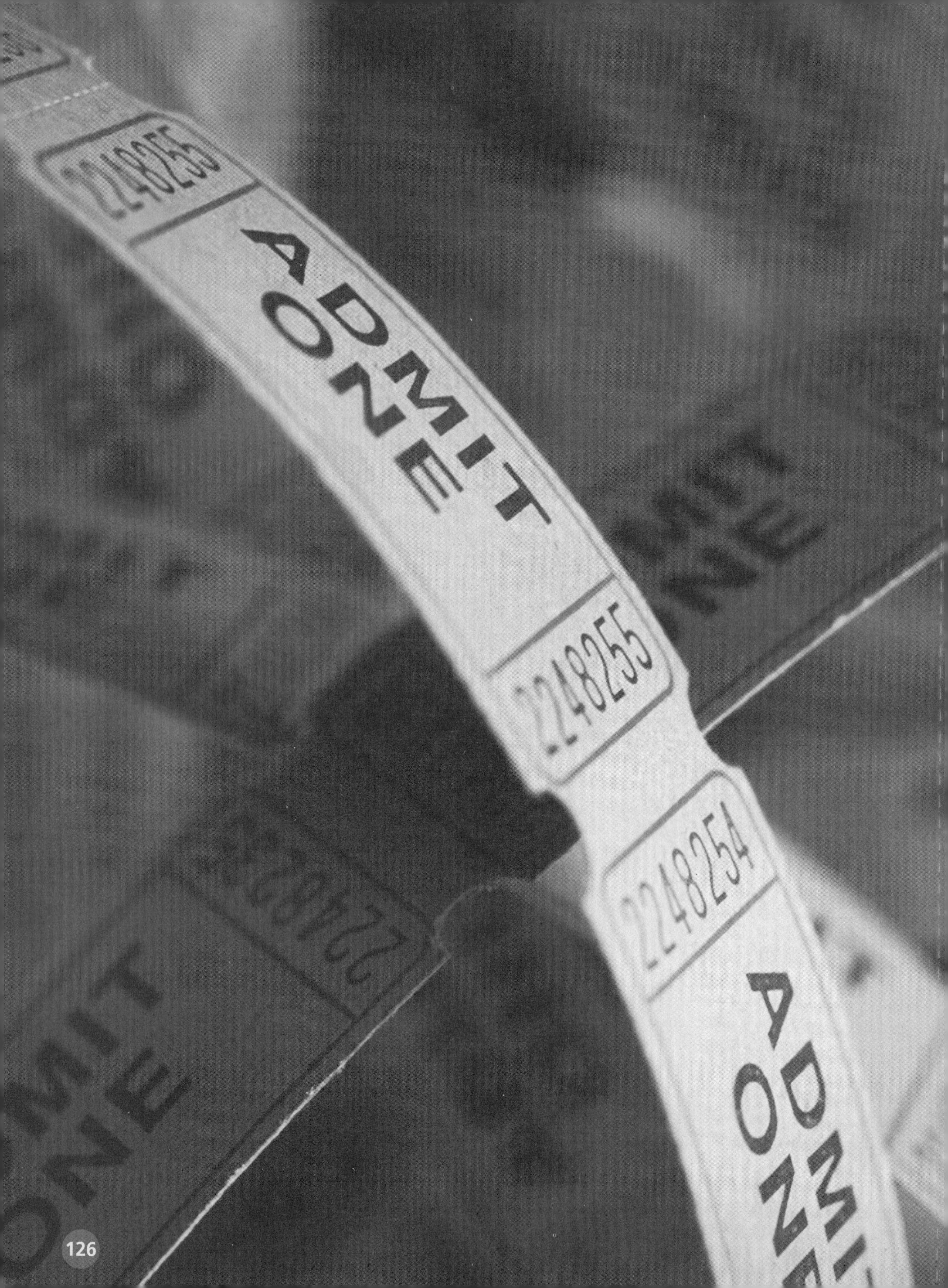
ADMIT ONE
2248255
2248255
2248254
ADMIT ONE

Name

# Crossword Pairs

Homophones The Spelling Words are pairs of homophones. **Homophones** are words that sound alike but have different spellings and meanings.

|sēn| seen    viewed; looked at

|sēn| scene    a short part of a play or movie

**Complete each puzzle with a pair of Spelling Words. Write the homophone that fits each meaning.**

## Spelling Words

1. seen
2. scene
3. wear
4. where
5. bow
6. bough
7. great
8. grate
9. fair
10. fare

### My Study List
What other words do you need to study for spelling? Add them to My Study List for *Felita* in the back of this book.

**Across**

2. part of a play or story
4. a large tree branch
6. to have on the body
8. according to the rules
10. terrific, remarkable

**Down**

1. viewed
3. to bend forward from the waist
5. at what place
7. money one must pay to travel
9. to rub against with a scraping sound

Name

# Spelling Spree

**Proofreading**  Find and circle five misspelled Spelling Words in this play script. Then write each word correctly.

| Spelling Words |
|---|
| 1. seen |
| 2. scene |
| 3. wear |
| 4. where |
| 5. bow |
| 6. bough |
| 7. great |
| 8. grate |
| 9. fair |
| 10. fare |

**PAPI:**  Tito, whare is the can of oil? Your bike wheels grait on their axles, and the sound is driving me crazy.

**TITO:**  Gee, Papi, I haven't sen it lately. Hey, Felita, can you find the oil can?

**FELITA:**  Do you think it's fare, Tito, for me to have to look for the things you've lost? After all—oh, here it is!

**PAPI:**  You're great at finding things, Felita! Take a bou!

**1** _____

**2** _____

**3** _____

**4** _____

**5** _____

**Hink Pinks**  Write the Spelling Word that fits each clue and rhymes with the given word.

**Example:** a burning wheel    **tire** ____fire____

**6**  a part of a play in which the actors are high school students    **teen** _____

**7**  a cattle-shaped tree branch    **cow** _____

**8**  the money a rabbit gives to a bus driver    **hare** _____

**9**  a remarkable wooden box  _____ **crate**

**10**  clothing for a female horse    **mare** _____

  **Tryout Tales**  Imagine that you tried out for a lead role in the school play. On a separate sheet of paper, write the telephone conversation you had with your best friend that evening. Include details about how you felt as you read, who else tried out, and how well you think you did. Use Spelling Words from the list.

Name

# Puerto Rico Calls!

**Linking Verbs** Tío Jorge likes to talk to Felita about Puerto
Rico. Create a travel brochure about the island. Pick the best
word or words from the box to complete each sentence.

subject    linking verb    predicate noun

**Puerto Rico is an island.**

linking verb

subject    predicate adjective

**The sea looks calm.**

delicious
swimmer
island
good
smell
spot
delightful
feel
special
taste
small
appears
homesick
beautiful

Puerto Rico _____ _____ on the map.
                   (linking verb)      (predicate adjective)

However, it is a beautiful _____ below Florida. The flowers
                                (predicate noun)

_____ so _____ there. The bananas
(linking verb)        (predicate adjective)

_____ really _____. The weather is
(linking verb)             (predicate adjective)

_____. The island is a perfect _____ for tourists.
(predicate adjective)                        (predicate noun)

The ocean looks _____ from the beaches. You will enjoy its beauty
                  (predicate adjective)

even if you are not a _____. Everyone's memories of Puerto Rico
                        (predicate noun)

are very _____. Once you have visited Puerto Rico, you will always
          (predicate adjective)

_____ _____ for our island!
(linking verb)      (predicate adjective)

Now write two sentences advertising Puerto Rico. Use a
linking verb in one and an action verb in the other.

**1** _____
                        (linking verb)

**2** _____
                        (action verb)

# Special Delivery

**Linking Verbs** Help Felita finish a letter she might write to Gigi. Pick the word or words you need to complete each sentence. Then complete the postscript by writing one sentence using a linking verb and one using an action verb.

| sorry | confident | looked | one | artist |
|-------|-----------|--------|-----|--------|
| fault | felt | fun | talented | angry |
| appeared | actress | happy | friends | |

Dear Gigi,

I am _____ about our fight. It was my _____.
    (predicate adjective)                                    (predicate noun)

I _____ _____ about the play. I wanted the
    (linking verb)    (predicate adjective)

part of Priscilla. But you were the best _____ for it. On stage
                                          (predicate pronoun)

you _____ calm and _____, not at all worried.
    (linking verb)              (predicate adjective)

You are a talented _____. I am _____ too. I am
                    (predicate noun)        (predicate adjective)

a good _____. My sets _____ almost real.
        (predicate noun)            (linking verb)

Now that we have talked, I am _____ again. We will always be
                              (predicate adjective)

_____!
(predicate noun)

Love,

*Felita*

P.S. The play was so much _____!
                          (predicate noun)

**❶** _____
                        (linking verb)

**❷** _____
                        (action verb)

Name

# Helping a Friend Get the Picture

Can you remember something that puzzled you when you saw it for the first time? Suppose you took Shirley someplace completely new to her. Imagine how things would look to her. Write a paragraph that tells about it.

**Where will you and Shirley go?**

___ We'll go to see the play that Felita's school is putting on.

___ We'll go to see T.J.'s team play ball.

___ We'll go to see _____

_____

Think about the actions or events that might seem strange to Shirley and list them in the chart.

| What Shirley saw | What Shirley thought she saw |
|---|---|
|  |  |
|  |  |
|  |  |

Pick one thing that puzzled Shirley. Write a paragraph telling what Shirley saw, what she thought she saw, and how you explained it. Share your paragraph with your class.

## Checklist

Before you share your paragraph, use this list to check your work.

❑ I picked something that Shirley could easily be confused by.

❑ I was able to explain to her what she really saw.

❑ My paragraph tells clearly what happened.

Name

# Catastrophe!

After you read each selection in Catastrophe!, complete
the chart below and on the next page.

| | The selection is an example of what kind of writing? | Describe the catastrophe featured in the selection. |
|---|---|---|
| Night of the Twisters | | |
| Earthquakes | | |
| The Story of the *Challenger* Disaster | | |

Name _____

# Catastrophe!

**After you read each selection in Catastrophe!, complete the chart.**

| | How do people in the selection react to catastrophe? | What did you learn about coping with catastrophes? |
|---|---|---|
| **Night of the Twisters** | | |
| **Earthquakes** | | |
| **The Story of the *Challenger* Disaster** | | |

If a disaster were to occur in your community, what would you do to help?

_____

_____

_____

# Picking Up the Pieces

A tornado has hit! Help your sister pick up the pieces. Cut out and paste them on another sheet of paper to create five of your sister's toys. On each toy, write a word from the box that has about the same meaning as the rest of the words.

| jolt | huddled | flickering | sobering | head-on | jammed |
|------|---------|------------|----------|---------|--------|

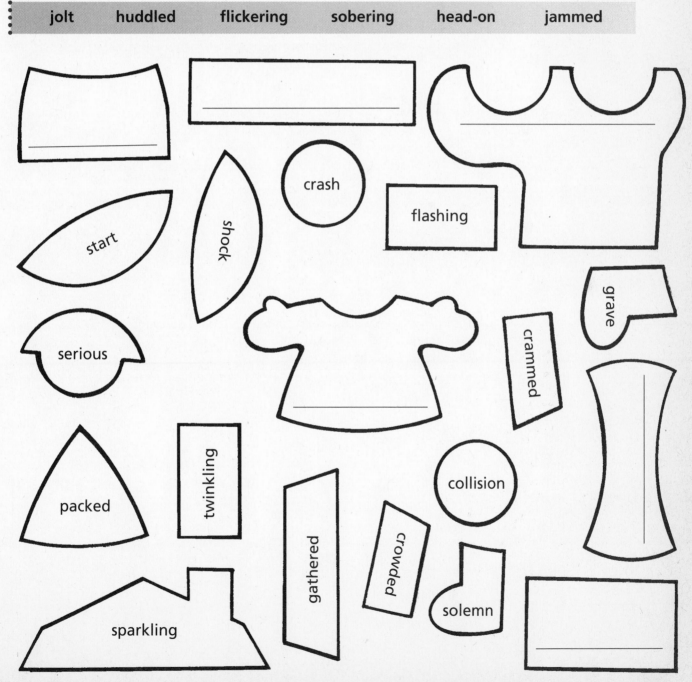

start

shock

crash

flashing

serious

grave

crammed

packed

twinkling

collision

gathered

crowded

solemn

sparkling

# A New Spin on the Story

These pictures show items or places in Dan's house. Next to each picture tell how the item or place played a part in what Dan, Arthur, or Ryan did during the tornado.

TORNADO ALERT

**1** _____
_____
_____
_____

**2** _____
_____
_____
_____

**3** _____
_____
_____
_____

**4** _____
_____
_____

**5** _____
_____
_____
_____

Name

# Twister Terror!

Complete the sentences to illustrate some of the cause-effect relationships in *Night of the Twisters.* Then show which part of each sentence is the cause and which is the effect by completing the chart.

**1** Dan calls his grandmother on the phone because _____

_____

**2** When the radio dies and the television flashes the emergency warning, Dan decides to _____

_____

**3** Arthur tries to run outside because _____

_____

**4** When Ryan gets tangled in the mobile, Dan can't _____

_____

### Cause

### Effect

**1** _____ | _____

**2** _____ | _____

**3** _____ | _____

**4** _____ | _____

Name _____

# Get the Scoop

Choose a recent event that you think would make a great news
article. Find out the facts. Conduct interviews, if possible. Record
your information on this page. Then use the information to write
your news article on a separate sheet of paper.

**Event:** _____

**What** happened?_____

_____

**When** did the event happen? _____

_____

**Where** did the event happen? _____

_____

**Why** did the event happen? _____

_____

**Who** was involved in the event? _____

_____

Whom can I **interview** about the event? _____

What are other **details** about the event?_____

_____

_____

_____

_____

_____

_____

 Catastrophe! **141**

Name ..............................................................

# Tornado Is to Twister as Fear Is to . . .

 is to  as  is to

**Look for similar relationships in analogies.**

**Write the best word to complete each analogy.**

**1** Tornado is to wind as flood is to _____.

storm   water   lifeboat

**2** Rain is to drop as snow is to _____.

cold   white   flake

**3** Hot is to sweat as cold is to _____.

sweater   chilly   shiver

**4** Harm is to damage as rush is to _____.

danger   hurry   late

**5** Chair is to sit as ladder is to _____.

climb   tall   paint

**6** Afraid is to fearless as cause is to _____.

reason   create   prevent

**7** Building is to basement as flower is to _____.

root   blossom   stem

**8** Shelter is to protect as shake is to _____.

collapse   tremble   steady

**9** Telephone is to talk as paper is to _____.

mailbox   write   letter

**10** Siren is to emergency as doorbell is to _____.

ring   door   visitor

# Tornado Terms

Match each word from the box with its definition. Write only one letter of the word in each blank. Then use the numbered letters to decode four names for kinds of tornadoes.

| startled |
| --- |
| sobering |
| scrambled |
| jammed |
| jolt |
| siren |
| huddled |
| flickering |
| deafening |
| head-on |

**1** blinking unsteadily

\_\_ \_\_ \_\_ \_\_ \_\_ \_\_ \_\_ \_\_ \_\_ \_\_
  13

**2** extremely loud    \_\_ \_\_ \_\_ \_\_ \_\_ \_\_ \_\_ \_\_ \_\_
                           8

**3** head-to-head collision    \_\_ \_\_ \_\_ \_\_ – \_\_ \_\_
             4

**4** a sudden jerk or shake; a shock or surprise    \_\_ \_\_ \_\_ \_\_
                1

**5** making one feel serious    \_\_ \_\_ \_\_ \_\_ \_\_ \_\_ \_\_ \_\_
          5         9

**6** surprised and somewhat frightened    \_\_ \_\_ \_\_ \_\_ \_\_ \_\_ \_\_ \_\_
          10

**7** a device that makes a loud warning noise    \_\_ \_\_ \_\_ \_\_ \_\_
       7      12

**8** packed tightly together; stuck    \_\_ \_\_ \_\_ \_\_ \_\_ \_\_
       11      3

**9** moved quickly, especially by crawling or climbing

\_\_ \_\_ \_\_ \_\_ \_\_ \_\_ \_\_ \_\_ \_\_
  2

**10** crowded or pushed closely together    \_\_ \_\_ \_\_ \_\_ \_\_ \_\_ \_\_
       6

1 \_\_   W
9 \_\_
7 \_\_
1 \_\_
12 \_\_
10 \_\_

2 \_\_   Y
2 \_\_
13 \_\_
5 \_\_
8 \_\_
12 \_\_

   W
4 \_\_
9 \_\_
10 \_\_
13 \_\_
   W
9 \_\_
8 \_\_
3 \_\_

   W
11 \_\_
1 \_\_
12 \_\_
10 \_\_
7 \_\_
   P
5 \_\_
6 \_\_
1 \_\_

# Cleanup Time

**Compound Words** Each Spelling Word is a compound word. A **compound word** is made up of two or more shorter words. Compound words can be written as one word, as a hyphenated word, or as separate words.

**hall** + **way** = hallway
**built** + **in** = built-in
**first** + **aid** = first aid

Help clean up the mess left by the tornado! Fill in the missing part of each compound word to form a Spelling Word. Then write the word under the correct heading.

## Spelling Words

1. hallway
2. upstairs
3. flashlight
4. everything
5. driveway

6. built-in
7. first aid
8. baby-sit
9. already
10. all right

### My Study List
What other words do you need to study for spelling? Add them to My Study List for *Night of the Twisters* in the back of this book.

drive_____

hall_____

_____stairs

baby_____

every_____

_____ right

built_____

_____light

_____aid

al_____

**One Word**

1 _____
2 _____
3 _____
4 _____
5 _____
6 _____

**Hyphenated Word**

7 _____
8 _____

**Separate Words**

9 _____
10 _____

Name

# Spelling Spree

**Safety Sense** Write a Spelling Word to complete each game card from a board game about safety.

**1** You list emergency phone numbers when you
_____
a neighbor's child.
**Move ahead 1 space.**

**3** You bandage your friend's sprained ankle because you know
_____.
**Take an extra turn.**

**2** You wait in the cellar as a tornado passes, so you are not hurt. You are
_____.
**Move ahead 3 spaces.**

**4** You leave your bike in the
_____.
Now your dad can't park the car.
**Lose 1 turn.**

**Proofreading** Find and circle six misspelled Spelling Words in this TV announcement. Then write each word correctly.

Spring's here alredy, so be prepared for tornado alerts! Buy fresh batteries for your falshlight and radio now. Also check your first aid supplies. Put evrything you'll need for an emergency in a handy spot like a hall-way closet or billt in cupboard. If you can keep spare supplies upstars too, so much the better. Know the safest spot in your home to wait out a twister. Be smart—be ready!

5 _____
6 _____
7 _____
8 _____
9 _____
10 _____

**Acrostic** Capture Dan's experience in a poem. Begin each line with a letter from the word *twister*. Tell what Dan felt, saw, and heard. The lines do not have to rhyme. Use Spelling Words from the list.

.............................................................
Name

# It Was Like This . . .

| **Singular** | **Plural** |
|---|---|
| A tornado <u>causes</u> much damage. | Tornadoes <u>cause</u> much damage. |
| It <u>approaches</u> rapidly. | They <u>approach</u> rapidly. |
| Dan <u>tries</u> his best. | Dan and Arthur <u>try</u> their best. |
| I <u>know</u> about tornadoes. | You <u>know</u> about tornadoes. |

**Subject-Verb Agreement** Arthur wants to appear on TV. Help
him finish his version of events for the producer. Write the correct
form of the verb shown in parentheses. Use the present tense.

**Example:** This memoir _____ tells _____ (tell) exactly what happened.

I _____ (recall) every second of that day. Here I am at my friend

Dan's house. Suddenly a siren _____ (blare) shrilly. Dan and I

_____ (know) that sound well. It _____

(mean) that a tornado is coming! Dan _____ (dash) to the telephone.

He _____ (try) his grandmother's number, but the phone line

_____ (buzz) loudly. I _____ (remain) calm,

but Dan _____ (become) more and more upset. Nervously he

_____ (watch) the TV screen. It _____ (flash)

the letters *CD, CD*. Then the lights and TV _____ (go) out. He

_____ (scream). Calmly I _____ (remind)

him about his baby brother. We _____ (hurry) upstairs to get Ryan.

Dan _____ (carry) the baby but does not know where to go.

"You _____ (remember)! The basement!" I

_____ (shout).

Name

# Help!

Singular
I **am** worried.
The <u>tornado</u> **is** close.

Plural
<u>We</u> **are** safe here.

**BE**

**HAVE**

Singular
I **have** a flashlight.
<u>It</u> **has** no batteries!

Plural
<u>We</u> **have** no food either.

**Subject-Verb Agreement** After the tornado, people placed newspaper ads. Finish them by adding the correct present tense forms of *be* and *have*. Then write one ad, using *be* or *have* in the present tense.

## Classified Ads

Lost dog! Rex _____ large and tan. His
<sub>be</sub>

tail and one ear _____ white. Please
<sub>be</sub>

call if you _____ the one who finds him.
<sub>be</sub>

If your water pipes _____ still broken,
<sub>be</sub>

call Polly the Plumber. She and her assistants

_____ the best you can _____.
<sub>be</sub> <sub>have</sub>

Be prepared for the next tornado! We

_____ flashlights for sale. Each light
<sub>have</sub>

_____ its own long-lasting batteries.
<sub>have</sub>

I _____ three pet iguanas. They
<sub>have</sub>

_____ no home right now. If you can
<sub>have</sub>

keep them until our house is rebuilt, please call.

I got lost in the storm. I _____ a small
<sub>be</sub>

orange-striped cat. My owners _____
<sub>be</sub>

lonely for me, I'm sure. Please come for me!

Tornado damage? If your dining table

_____ a broken leg or if you _____
<sub>have</sub> <sub>have</sub>

any other damaged furniture, call us for repairs!

Name _____

# Quake with These Words

**Follow the directions in each box. Then answer the questions in complete sentences using the underlined words.**

**1** Draw a picture of two objects colliding. Then write a caption using the word *colliding*.

_____
_____

**2** Show what happens to boats when the ocean heaves. Then write a caption using the word *heaves*.

_____
_____

**3** What happens when there is <u>friction</u> between two objects?

_____
_____

**4** Why do you think <u>stresses</u> weaken or change the shape of something?

_____
_____

**5** Where do you think <u>strains</u> can occur?

_____
_____

Name

# You're the Expert

You are Dr. Rocky Tremble. You plan to give a speech that answers commonly asked questions about earthquakes. Fill in the note cards.

**1** What causes an earthquake?

**2** What is the difference between the movement of a dip-slip fault and a strike-slip fault?

**3** Where do most of the earthquakes in the United States occur? Why?

**4** What should you do if an earthquake occurs when you are indoors?

**5** What should you do if you are outside during an earthquake?

**6** Why are seismographs important tools?

Name

# Generally Speaking

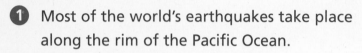

Read each of the statements. Circle each accurate
generalization, and list a fact from the selection that
supports it. Explain why the statements you left uncircled
are overgeneralizations.

**1** Most of the world's earthquakes take place
along the rim of the Pacific Ocean.

_____

_____

**2** Many earthquakes are destructive.

_____

_____

**3** Earthquakes in densely populated areas are always dangerous.

_____

_____

Now make a generalization about which structure would be more
likely to survive an earthquake. Use facts from the selection.

**Name:** Rose Towers
Apartments
**Location:** Southern
Florida
Built on solid rock

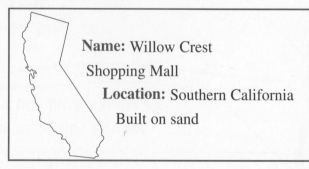

**Name:** Willow Crest
Shopping Mall
**Location:** Southern California
Built on sand

_____

_____

_____

_____

Name

# Use Your Own Words

Read the following article. Then paraphrase it
on the lines below.

## THE SAN FRANCISCO EARTHQUAKE OF 1989

It was 5:04 P.M. on the afternoon of October 17, 1989. At San
Francisco's Candlestick Park, the third game of the World Series was
about to begin. The two teams in the playoffs, the San Francisco Giants
and the Oakland Athletics, had just finished batting practice. People were
crowding into the stadium to watch their heroes play. Without warning,
the ground and bleachers began to shake, a rumbling was heard, and
chunks of concrete fell from the balconies.

Luckily, no one was injured at Candlestick Park, but that wasn't the
case elsewhere in the San Francisco area. The quake had lasted a mere
fifteen seconds but had caused a lot of damage. In West Oakland, the top
half of a double-decker highway collapsed. Many buildings in the Marina
District were destroyed, and a section of the Oakland Bay Bridge collapsed.

Despite the damage and the human lives that were lost, many
parts of San Francisco looked untouched by the quake.

# Word Shake-Up

Write the word from the box that completes each sentence. If the word contains the word root *struct*, write the tinted letter on the house part labeled STRUCT. If the word contains the word root *rupt*, write the tinted letter on the house part labeled RUPT. Then unscramble the letters and complete the sentence at the bottom of the page.

| bankrupt | instructions | structure | erupt |
|---|---|---|---|
| destruction | disrupted | construction | obstructing |

**1** A big earthquake can cause terrible _____.

__ __ __ __ __ __ __ __ __ __

**2** During an emergency, follow _____.

__ __ __ __ __ __ __ __ __ __ __ __

**3** The damage to our home _____ our lives.

__ __ __ __ __ __ __ __

**4** A fallen telephone pole was _____ traffic.

__ __ __ __ __ __ __ __ __ __ __

**5** The _____ workers repaired the apartment building.

__ __ __ __ __ __ __ __ __ __ __ __

**6** When their shop was destroyed, they were left _____.

__ __ __ __ __ __ __ __

**7** An earthquake can cause "sand boils" to _____ from the ground.

__ __ __ __ __

**8** A building must have a strong _____ to withstand earthquakes.

__ __ __ __ __ __ __ __ __

STRUCT

H

C

RUPT

L

C

Something that scientists use to measure earthquakes is

the _____ _____.

# Rebuild the Building!

Repair the earthquake damage. Cut out the boxes at the foot of the page and paste them on the left side of the building. Match each vocabulary word with its definition. Then, on the back of this paper, write a short article about the earthquake. Use at least five vocabulary words.

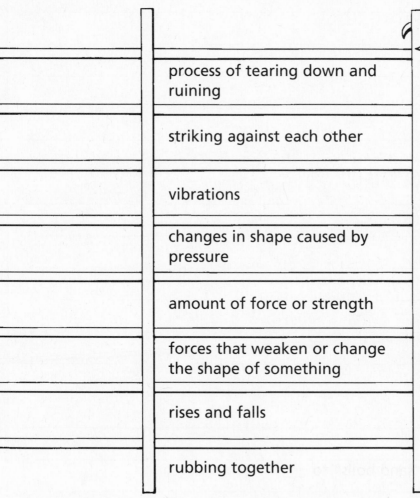

process of tearing down and ruining

striking against each other

vibrations

changes in shape caused by pressure

amount of force or strength

forces that weaken or change the shape of something

rises and falls

rubbing together

| tremors | destruction | friction | strains |
| colliding | intensity | heaves | stresses |

**Write a short article about the earthquake. Use at least five vocabulary words.**

_____

_____

_____

_____

_____

_____

_____

_____

_____

_____

_____

_____

_____

_____

_____

_____

_____

_____

# Shake, Rattle, and Roll

**The VCCV and VCV Patterns** Each
Spelling Word has two syllables. Some Spelling
Words have the vowel-consonant-consonant-
vowel (VCCV) pattern. To find the syllables in
most **VCCV** words, divide the word
between the consonants.

## Spelling Words

1. damage
2. surface
3. entire
4. solid
5. total
6. object
7. notice
8. suffer
9. modern
10. mirror

### My Study List
What other words do you
need to study for spelling?
Add them to My Study List for
Earthquakes in the back of this book.

VC|CV
suf|fer

VC|CV
sur|face

The other Spelling Words have the vowel-
consonant-vowel (VCV) pattern. VCV words
are usually divided before the consonant if
the first syllable has a long vowel sound and
after the consonant if the first syllable has a
short vowel sound. Divide each word before
or after the consonant.

Write each Spelling Word under the correct pattern.
Then draw a line dividing each word into syllables.

V|CV
to|t al

VC|V
dam|age

**VCCV**

1. _____
2. _____
3. _____
4. _____
5. _____

**VCV**

6. _____
7. _____
8. _____
9. _____
10. _____

# Spelling Spree

**Proofreading** Find and circle six misspelled Spelling Words. Then write each word correctly.

| Spelling Words |
|---|
| 1. damage |
| 2. surface |
| 3. entire |
| 4. solid |
| 5. total |
| 6. object |
| 7. notice |
| 8. suffer |
| 9. modern |
| 10. mirror |

Almost 2000 years ago a Chinese scientist invented an "earthquake alarm." Like modurn seismographs, it recorded movements of the earth's surfus. Eight dragon heads jutted out from the kettle-like objekt. Each head held a soled metal ball, and a toad sat below. When the ground shook, the ball dropped into the toad's open mouth with a clang the scientist was sure to nottis!! Thus, he knew that somewhere in China, people had suffered earthquake dammage.

1 _____  3 _____  5 _____

2 _____  4 _____  6 _____

**Headlines** Replace the underlined words in each newspaper headline with a Spelling Word having a similar meaning. Remember to use a capital letter.

7. **Reflective Glass Shatters, Misses Sleeping Child**

8. Power Losses Affect Whole City

9. **Troy and Eltown Experience Quake Destruction**

10. Added-up Cost of Quake Repair Reaches Millions

7 _____

8 _____

9 _____

10 _____

**Disaster Relief** Natural disasters can change people's lives forever. Can you help those people get back to normal? On a separate sheet of paper, list four practical ways to help. Use Spelling Words from the list.

Name

# New! Improved!

| Past Tense | Present Tense | Future Tense |
|---|---|---|
| Yesterday experts **predicted** a quake. | Now the tremors **shake** us. | Soon we **will repair** our house. |

**Verb Tenses**  An inventor wants a patent on her new, improved earthquake-measuring machine. Help her fill out a patent application. Write the verb in the present, the past, or the future tense.

| National Patent Office Application for a Patent | |
|---|---|
| **Name of machine:** | The Seismic Wonder |
| **Purpose:** | to measure the force of earthquake tremors |

**Explanation:**

Five years ago I _____ (notice) problems with earthquake-measuring

scales. Immediately, I _____ (start) work on my own machine. Now it is

ready. Soon other machines _____ (become) useless.

The Seismic Wonder is remarkable. In tests last year, it _____

(perform) amazingly well. When it was tested in China, it _____ (record)

seismic shocks within a second. When it was tested in California, it

_____ (measure) slips in the San Andreas fault perfectly. The parts of

the Seismic Wonder are simple. They _____ (shift) through water to

measure the smallest movement. As you watch, the needles _____

(swing) to the correct number on the dial.

In the coming years, the Seismic Wonder _____ (change) earthquake

measurement forever. Everyone _____ (use) this remarkable instrument.

............................................

Name

# Tense Situation

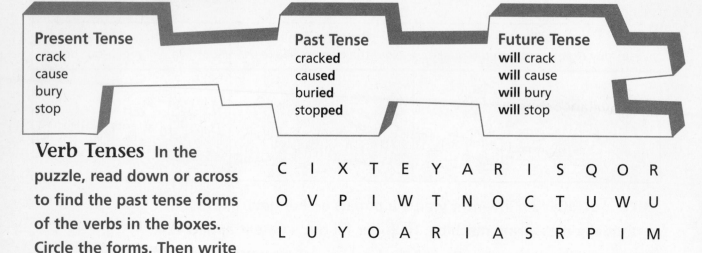

| Present Tense | Past Tense | Future Tense |
|---|---|---|
| crack | crack**ed** | **will** crack |
| cause | caus**ed** | **will** cause |
| bury | bur**ied** | **will** bury |
| stop | stop**ped** | **will** stop |

**Verb Tenses** In the puzzle, read down or across to find the past tense forms of the verbs in the boxes. Circle the forms. Then write them on the lines.

carry

roar

rumble

snap

collapse

push

stretch

try

shout

grab

```
C I X T E Y A R I S Q O R
O V P I W T N O C T U W U
L U Y O A R I A S R P I M
L T I U W I X R P E O O B
A N Q I O E Y E O T C D L
P U S H E D U D V C B L E
S M Y P T I W K N H I P D
E N G O S H O U T E D I G
D N J C A R R I E D P O K
Y S N A P P E D Y O V F F
U P K C V O G R A B B E D
```

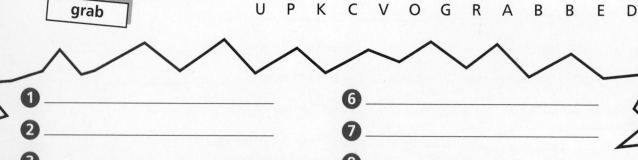

1. _____  6. _____
2. _____  7. _____
3. _____  8. _____
4. _____  9. _____
5. _____  10. _____

**More!** On another sheet of paper, write a short poem about an earthquake. Use at least five of the past tense forms.

Name _____

# I Wonder Why . . .

**Report Topics**  Are you curious about one of these topics?
What other ones do they make you think of?

avalanches
poisonous insects
Boston Tea Party
cotton
training for a marathon
scuba diving

Sojourner Truth
weather forecasting
The Great Wall of China
Klondike Gold Rush
Kamehameha the Great

**My Report Topics**  Write five ideas that you might like to write about in a report.

**1** _____

**2** _____

**3** _____

**4** _____

**5** _____

Ask yourself these questions about each idea you listed.

Can I find information
about it easily?

Can I cover it in a
short report, or do I need
to narrow the topic?

Am I really interested in
writing about this?

Now circle the topic that you will
write about. You may want to
check your library resources
before you decide.

# Be a Researcher

Write your report topic. Then fill in the first two columns of the chart to help you plan your research. In the column "What I Want to Know," write questions you would like to answer about your topic. Fill in the last column later when you have finished your report.

**My Topic** _____

| What I Know | What I Want to Know | What I Learned |
|---|---|---|
| | | |

Name

# Taking Another Look

Reread and revise your report, using the Revising Checklist. Then use the Questions for a Writing Conference to help you discuss your report with a classmate.

## Revising Checklist

☐ Have I stated my main ideas in topic sentences?

☐ Do all the facts in each paragraph support the main idea?

☐ Where should I add more information?

☐ Have I used my own words?

☐ Does my introduction prepare the reader for the report?

☐ Does my conclusion sum up the report?

## Questions for a Writing Conference

• What do you like about this report?

• Does any part seem unclear? Why? Not enough facts? Unfamiliar words?

• Do any facts belong in other parts of the report?

• Do any parts seem out of order?

• Does any information seem not to belong?

• How could the introduction or conclusion be improved?

## My Notes
Write notes to remember ideas discussed in your writing conference.

_____

_____

_____

_____

_____

_____

_____

_____

Name

# A Tribute to Challenger

Use the vocabulary words to complete the
plaque. Then answer the question.

| | |
|---|---|
| commemorate | grief |
| tragedy | mourned |
| sympathy | memorial |

This plaque is a _____ to the seven
astronauts killed January 28, 1986, when the space shuttle
*Challenger* exploded shortly after takeoff. It was created
to _____ the seven brave heroes who lost their
lives. As a nation, we _____ the loss of *Challenger*.
We expressed sadness and _____ over the deaths
of the *Challenger* crew. We send our _____ to
the families and friends of those seven brave astronauts who
sacrificed their lives for science. The *Challenger* explosion is a
_____ we will never forget.

What kind of tribute would you make to honor the astronauts
killed in the *Challenger* disaster?

_____

_____

_____

_____

_____

Name _____

# Countdown to Disaster

Explain the sequence of events surrounding the *Challenger* disaster by completing the sentences. Then answer the question.

Christa McAuliffe is chosen to be the first

McAuliffe travels to the Johnson Space Center, where she

meets and trains with

The launch of the shuttle is delayed for three days because of

Seventy-four seconds after the *Challenger* is launched, it

Rescue efforts are attempted, but

People show their grief for the astronauts who died by

**How did you feel when you read the description of the *Challenger* explosion?**

_____

_____

_____

_____

# Think for Yourself

Draw conclusions by answering the questions in the charts.

**Facts**

How did Christa McAuliffe react to being chosen to ride in the space shuttle?

**Personal Experiences**

How would you feel if you were chosen?

**Conclusion**

What would it be like to be chosen to ride the space shuttle?

**Facts**

How did students react to the disaster?

**Personal Experiences**

How did you feel as you read about the shuttle explosion?

**Conclusion**

What would it have been like to be one of Christa McAuliffe's students?

# A Business Matter

Use this page to help you plan your business letter.

**Inside address**

Name of person who will
receive letter (and his or her title): _____

Company name (if there is one): _____

Address: _____

_____

**Greeting**

Person's name or a general greeting: _____

**Body**

Purpose of letter: _____

_____

Details I need to include: _____

_____

_____

_____

**Closing**

_____

Name

# Compound Challenge

Each word in the box is a compound word made up of two smaller words. Search for the "word within a word" that matches each puzzle clue. Then complete the crossword puzzle.

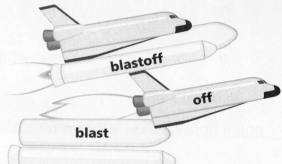

blastoff

off

blast

**Across**

3. wide
6. move swiftly
7. looking
8. road
9. the sun, for example
12. soil *or* our planet
14. to throw
16. opposite of forward
18. where birds fly
19. without leaks

skyrocket
stargazing
broadcast
earthbound
breathtaking
setback
airtight
runway
moonlight
safeguard

**Down**

1. to protect
2. Earth has only one.
3. tied *or* headed
4. brightness
5. air inhaled and exhaled
10. craft that shoots into space
11. put
13. opposite of giving
15. not dangerous
17. contains oxygen

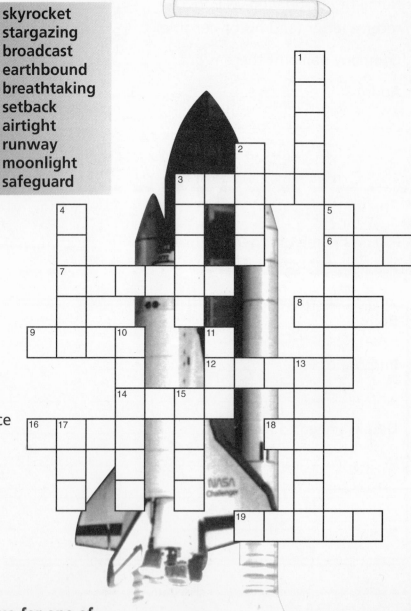

**More!** Write a crossword clue for one of the two words that make up the compound word *blastoff*.

Name

# In Honor of *Challenger*

Take a moment to remember the *Challenger* crew. Write each vocabulary word next to its definition. Then use at least five vocabulary words to write a paragraph or a poem honoring the *Challenger* astronauts.

**1** deep sadness caused by disaster or loss _____

**2** suddenly surprised or upset _____

**3** something that is put up, kept, or done to help people remember a person or event _____

**4** to honor the memory of someone or something _____

**5** to feel or express sorrow for someone who has died _____

**6** very sad event; terrible happening _____

**7** bad luck _____

**8** unwillingness to accept that something is true _____

**9** expression of sorrow for the sadness of another person _____

**10** something given or done to show respect or thanks _____

| misfortune    commemorate<br>tragedy    grief<br>tribute    shocked<br>memorial    disbelief<br>sympathy    mourn | |
|---|---|
|  |  |
|  |  |

Name

# On to the Stars

**The VCCCV Pattern** Each two-syllable Spelling Word has the vowel-consonant-consonant-consonant-vowel (VCCCV) pattern. In each word, two different consonants spell one sound (as in *farther*) or form a cluster (as in *explode*). Divide each word into syllables before or after those two consonants. Look for familiar patterns, and spell the word by syllables.

**My Study List**
What other words do you need to study for spelling? Add them to My Study List for *The Story of the Challenger Disaster* in the back of this book.

VC | CCV:    far | ther
VCC | CV:   sand | wich
VC | CCV:    ex | plode

**Find the Spelling Word that fits each clue, and write it under the correct heading. Then draw a line dividing each word into syllables.**

**Clues**

1. two or more slices of bread with a food filling
2. containing nothing
3. at a greater distance
4. brief moment
5. to search for
6. to put into words
7. great effort
8. to speak to; to greet
9. to burst suddenly
10. power that checks and regulates an operation

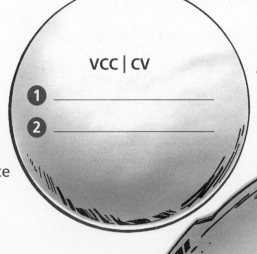

**VCC | CV**

1 _____

2 _____

**VC | CCV**

3 _____

4 _____

5 _____

6 _____

7 _____

8 _____

9 _____

10 _____

# Spelling Spree

**Proofreading** Find and circle five misspelled Spelling Words on this monument. Then write each word correctly.

## Spelling Words

1. explode
2. instant
3. control
4. explore
5. address
6. struggle
7. express
8. empty
9. farther
10. sandwich

We dedicate this monument to those brave souls who traveled ever farthur from Earth and reached ever higher to achieve the impossible. Some missions failed in an instent; others succeeded only after years of strugle. Our space pioneers risked their lives to explor and settle the empty reaches of space. To all those who showed commitment and courage, we espres our heartfelt thanks. Touch the stars!

**1** _____

**2** _____

**3** _____

**4** _____

**5** _____

## Analogies Write a Spelling Word to complete each analogy.

**Example:** Close is to distant as nearer is to farther.

**6** Occupied is to full as unoccupied is to _____.

**7** Book covers are to book as bread slices are to _____.

**8** Fence is to limit as leash is to _____.

**9** Volcano is to erupt as bomb is to _____.

**10** Greeting is to welcome as speech is to _____.

**No Limit to Dreams** Imagine it is the year 2150. What has the space program achieved since the *Challenger* disaster? On a separate sheet of paper, write a brief news story about the latest space mission. Explain the mission's purpose. Use Spelling Words from the list.

Name

# Space Camp

|  | Verb | Past Tense | | Past with Helping Verb |
|---|---|---|---|---|
| **Regular** | look | looked | | (has, have, had) looked |
| **Irregular** | see | saw | | (has, have, had) seen |
| | go | went | | (has, have, had) gone |

**Irregular Verbs** You are a news reporter interviewing an astronaut
in training. For each question, write a response using the past tense
form of the highlighted verb or the past tense with a helping verb.

**Example:**

**Q.** Did you **write** an application for this training camp?

**A.** I **wrote** an application and also went to an interview.

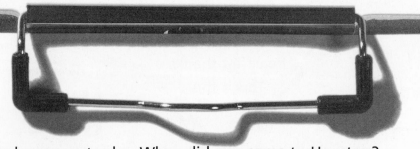

**Q.** Training camp began yesterday. When did you **come** to Houston?

**A.** _____

**Q.** Do the officers **make** you work hard?

**A.** They have _____

**Q.** Did you **go** on any training flights?

**A.** _____

**Q.** Do you **take** any tests during training camp?

**A.** Yes, I have _____

**Q.** When you were a kid, what did you **think** of space travel?

**A.** _____

**Q.** Will you **write** about your training experience?

**A.** Yes; in fact, I have _____

Name _____

# Wish You Were Here!

**Irregular Verbs** Your dream came true! You saw a shuttle launch in person. Write a post card describing the experience to a friend. Use five verbs from the box in the past tense form or the past with a helping verb.

| bring | run | take | come | make |
|-------|-----|------|------|------|
| think | go | see | write | say |

Place
Stamp
Here

To: _____

_____

_____

Name ...................................................................

# Dealing with an Emergency

You know that people can get frightened and confused in an emergency. Planning and cool thinking are important for survival. Make a chart and a display that explain what can happen if people act correctly or incorrectly when disaster strikes.

First, pick a kind of emergency that you are familiar with.

The emergency: _____

How might people react to the things that happen? Give examples of a smart action and a foolish action. Then give the likely results of each action. (You may want to make a chart like this on a separate sheet of paper.)

| What Happens | How People React | | The Results |
|---|---|---|---|
| | good: | | |
| | bad: | | |
| | good: | | |
| | bad: | | |
| | good: | | |
| | bad: | | |

Turn your chart into a mobile. Write the "What Happens" events on tag-board cards and attach them to a coat hanger. On separate cards, write responses to the events and the results of the responses. Have one of your group present your work to the class.

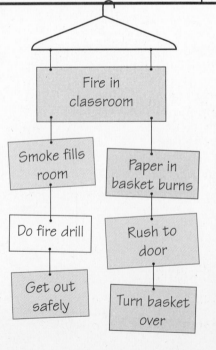

### Revising Checklist

☐ We picked a common emergency and described what it might involve.

☐ We explained how people might try to cope with the emergency.

☐ We explained the likely results of their actions.

Name

# From the Prairie to the Sea

Complete the chart below and on the next page with information from each selection. Then use that information to answer the questions.

| | What problems or challenges did the characters face? | What did the characters do for fun or for pleasure? |
|---|---|---|
| **Along the Santa Fe Trail** | | |
| **Children of the Wild West** | | |
| **Pecos Bill** | | |

For the characters you have read about, do you think the hardships outweighed the benefits of living in the West in the 1800s? Explain your answer.

_____

_____

Name .....................................................

# From the Prairie to the Sea

Complete the chart with information from each selection. Then use
that information to answer the questions.

| | How did the characters change throughout the story? | What were the attitudes of the characters toward the West? |
|---|---|---|
| Along the Santa Fe Trail | | |
| Children of the Wild West | | |
| Pecos Bill | | |

Based on the characters you have read about, how important was the land and the
surroundings in the West to the people who lived there? Explain your answer.

_____

_____

# Trail Words

Write each word from the box on the correct line.

| caravan | vast | desolate | mesa | epidemic | wallows | emigrant |

**sights**
_____
_____

**transportation**
_____
_____

**description**
_____
_____

**travelers**
_____
_____

**dangers**
_____
_____

Traveling the Santa Fe Trail

Now choose at least three words from the box. Use them to write a
short paragraph describing a journey to the West in a covered wagon.

_____
_____
_____
_____
_____
_____
_____

Name

# Rating the Trail

Use information from *Along the Santa Fe Trail* to complete Marion's report of the trip.

## CONESTOGAS, INC.
### Customer Satisfaction Survey

Trail you took: _____

Leader of your caravan: _____

Traveling companions: _____

_____

Typical daytime schedule: _____

_____

Typical evening activities: _____

_____

Most exciting parts of trip: _____

_____

Most frightening parts of trip: _____

_____

Did you reach your destination?   ☐ yes      ☐ no

If not, why? _____

_____

Current residence: _____

Overall rating of Conestogas, Inc.:

☐ excellent      ☐ good      ☐ fair      ☐ poor

Name _____

# Propaganda Out West

TAKE THE SANTA FE TRAIL TO CALIFORNIA

**Take the Santa Fe Trail to California. It's safe and beautiful. On a recent journey, the weather was beautiful, and the travelers arrived in Santa Fe in record time.**

Everyone is getting rich in California! You can too! Mr. Edward Walsh, a mining expert, says,

"The gold in California is so plentiful that you can find gold nuggets in no time!"

Find an example of each type of propaganda on the posters. Write the example after each propaganda technique.

**1** Omission of facts: _____

_____

**2** Overgeneralization: _____

_____

**3** Bandwagon: _____

_____

**4** Testimonial: _____

_____

Now write a propaganda statement of your own. Your goal is to make people stay in the East or the Midwest and not travel on the Santa Fe Trail. Write the statement and then tell which technique you used.

**5** _____

_____

# I'll Answer That

Circle an essay question that you would like to write about. Use the
space below to plan and write your answer.

> **A.** Explain the advantages and disadvantages of traveling in a wagon train.
> Use details from *Along the Santa Fe Trail* to support your answer.
> **B.** Describe and discuss some of the things the narrator enjoyed about
> traveling on the Santa Fe Trail.
> **C.** Compare and contrast the narrator and her brother, Will.

**1** Are there any key words in the question? If so, what are they? _____

_____

**2** Plan your answer: _____

_____

_____

_____

**3** Write your response to the question: _____

_____

_____

_____

_____

_____

_____

_____

_____

Name ..................................................................

# Spectacular Westward Transportation!

| spec (root) | tacular | | trans | port (root) | ation |

Some words in the covered wagon contain the word root *port*, which means "carry." Others contain the word root *spec*, which means "look." Write the words that match each clue. Then write each numbered letter in the space with the matching number to find a message.

**1** <u>looked</u> at closely for problems or mistakes

$\underline{\phantom{x}}_{5} \ \underline{\phantom{x}}_{11} \ \underline{\phantom{x}} \ \underline{\phantom{x}} \ \underline{\phantom{x}} \ \underline{\phantom{x}} \ \underline{\phantom{x}} \ \underline{\phantom{x}}_{8}$

**2** describes something you can <u>carry</u>

$\underline{\phantom{x}} \ \underline{\phantom{x}} \ \underline{\phantom{x}}_{6} \ \underline{\phantom{x}} \ \underline{\phantom{x}} \ \underline{\phantom{x}}$

**3** describes something fantastic to <u>look</u> at

$\underline{\phantom{x}} \ \underline{\phantom{x}} \ \underline{\phantom{x}}_{10} \ \underline{\phantom{x}} \ \underline{\phantom{x}}_{7} \ \underline{\phantom{x}} \ \underline{\phantom{x}} \ \underline{\phantom{x}} \ \underline{\phantom{x}}$

**4** someone paid to <u>carry</u> back information about an event

$\underline{\phantom{x}} \ \underline{\phantom{x}} \ \underline{\phantom{x}} \ \underline{\phantom{x}}_{4} \ \underline{\phantom{x}} \ \underline{\phantom{x}} \ \underline{\phantom{x}}$

**5** a point of view or way of <u>looking</u> at something

$\underline{\phantom{x}}_{15} \ \underline{\phantom{x}} \ \underline{\phantom{x}} \ \underline{\phantom{x}} \ \underline{\phantom{x}} \ \underline{\phantom{x}} \ \underline{\phantom{x}} \ \underline{\phantom{x}}_{3} \ \underline{\phantom{x}}_{9} \ \underline{\phantom{x}}$

**6** someone who <u>looks</u> on at an event

$\underline{\phantom{x}} \ \underline{\phantom{x}}_{2} \ \underline{\phantom{x}} \ \underline{\phantom{x}} \ \underline{\phantom{x}} \ \underline{\phantom{x}} \ \underline{\phantom{x}} \ \underline{\phantom{x}} \ \underline{\phantom{x}}_{14}$

**7** to <u>carry</u> the weight of something

$\underline{\phantom{x}}_{1} \ \underline{\phantom{x}}_{13} \ \underline{\phantom{x}} \ \underline{\phantom{x}} \ \underline{\phantom{x}} \ \underline{\phantom{x}}_{12} \ \underline{\phantom{x}}$

Those who traveled the Santa Fe Trail needed

a $\underline{\phantom{x}}_{1} \ \underline{\phantom{x}}_{2} \ \underline{\phantom{x}}_{3} \ \underline{\phantom{x}}_{4} \ \underline{\phantom{x}}_{5} \ \underline{\phantom{x}}_{6}$ of $\underline{\phantom{x}}_{7} \ \underline{\phantom{x}}_{8} \ \underline{\phantom{x}}_{9} \ \underline{\phantom{x}}_{10} \ \underline{\phantom{x}}_{11} \ \underline{\phantom{x}}_{12} \ \underline{\phantom{x}}_{13} \ \underline{\phantom{x}}_{14} \ \underline{\phantom{x}}_{15}$!

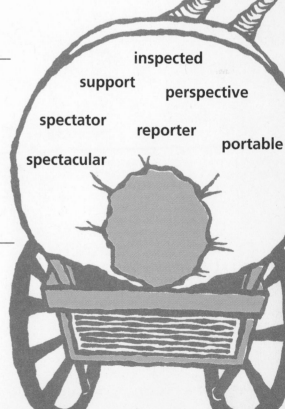

inspected

support

perspective

spectator

reporter

portable

spectacular

Name

# Travel the Santa Fe Trail!

You are a traveler on the Santa Fe Trail. Pause at the landmarks listed below to write one-sentence journal entries about your experiences. Use the vocabulary words in the box.

| | | |
|---|---|---|
| epidemic | corral | en route |
| caravan | turbulent | wallows |
| emigrant | mesa | desolate |
| plaza | | |

Name

# Wagon Words

**Adding *-ed* or *-ing*** Each Spelling Word is made up of a base word and an ending. A **base word** is a word to which a beginning or an ending can be added. When a base word ends with **e**, drop the **e** when adding **-ed** or **-ing**.

decide + ed = decided     stare + ing = staring

When a one-syllable word ends with one vowel and a single consonant, the consonant usually is doubled when **-ed** or **-ing** is added. When **-ed** or **-ing** is added to a two-syllable word, the consonant usually is not doubled.

plan + ing = planning     depart + ed = departed

Change the base words on the buckets into Spelling Words. Decide whether or not each base word has a spelling change when an **-ed** or **-ing** is added. Then write the Spelling Word formed from each base word on the correct wagon.

## Spelling Words

1. planning
2. decided
3. departed
4. staring
5. offered
6. slipping
7. numbered
8. scattered
9. healing
10. knitted

**My Study List**
What other words do you need to study for spelling? Add them to My Study List for *Along the Santa Fe Trail* in the back of this book.

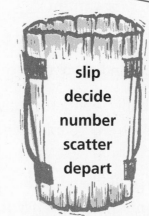

slip
decide
number
scatter
depart

stare
offer
heal
plan
knit

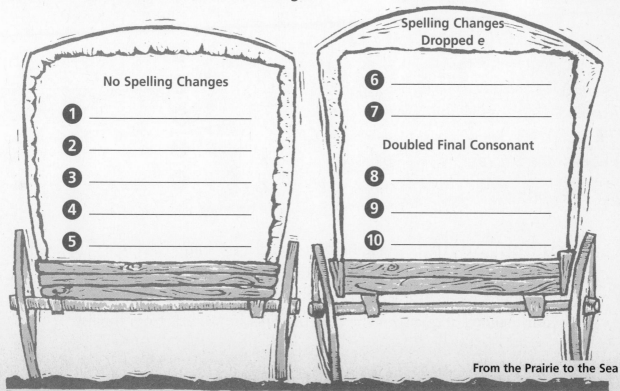

**No Spelling Changes**

1 _____
2 _____
3 _____
4 _____
5 _____

**Spelling Changes Dropped e**

6 _____
7 _____

**Doubled Final Consonant**

8 _____
9 _____
10 _____

.................................................................
Name

# Spelling Spree

**Trail Talk**  Write a Spelling Word to complete this conversation between two wagon train mules.

**Hee:** Mrs. W has _____ two hats and a sweater already!

**Haw:** Yes, but she's missing all the sights, such as the flowers _____ throughout the grass.  They make me hungry.

**Hee:** Say, when do we stop for lunch?  Soon, I hope.

**Haw:** I'm looking forward to _____ out of this harness.

**Hee:** That herd of buffalo we just passed probably _____ over a thousand. And all of them kept _____ at us.

**Haw:** They probably wondered why we're pulling this wagon but were too shy to ask! Heeee-hawwwwwwwwwwwww!

**Proofreading**  Find and circle five misspelled Spelling Words on this poster.  Write each word correctly.

## GOODS FOR SALE

To be ofered by Captain Dunn at a fair price, which will be desided the day of sale!  He departid Kansas by wagon train in April and is planing to arrive here in five weeks.  Goods will include buckles, needles, and other metal pieces (numbered at over 500) as well as cloth and medicine for heeling pains and fever.

**1** _____

**2** _____

**3** _____

**4** _____

**5** _____

**Snappy Sayings**  Imagine that you are traveling west in a covered wagon in 1852. On a separate sheet of paper, design three "bumper stickers" for your wagon. Each message should tell about your feelings or goals for the trip. Use Spelling Words from the list.

Name

# The Way West

**Punctuating Dialogue** Read this conversation. Notice
how the dialogue is punctuated.

> "What would you take with you in a covered wagon?"
> Louis asked.
> "I'd take all my favorite foods," Maria replied, "and
> plenty of water."
> Sarah said, "You would need blankets to stay warm."
> "I'd take a telephone," Chris added. "I could call for
> extra supplies."
> "The emigrants did not have telephones!" Louis
> exclaimed.

Add the correct punctuation to Aja's story about a wagon train traveling west. Use
proofreading marks to show her where to indent (¶), where to insert punctuation
(‸), and which letters to capitalize (≡). Then, on a separate sheet of paper, copy the
dialogue. Show the correct indents, punctuation, and capital letters.

**Example:** ¶ "how high the river is!" cried little Tad. ¶ "what shall
we do?" asked Sarah.

we can't drive the wagons across   said Father.   we'll have to

make a ferry.   what does that mean   asked Sarah.

it means   said Father   that we'll pull our wagon back and

forth across the river with long ropes. Once we unload our

things, our wagon will be a ferry for others.   will our wagon

carry other wagons   asked Tad.   they'll be emptied, taken

apart, and carried across in pieces   said Father.

# Western Word Search

**Punctuating Dialogue**  Find the words in the puzzle. They
run across, down, and diagonally. Then use at least six of the
words to write sentences that include direct quotations.

```
A O T P R A I R I E L D
D W R B U F T A M J R R
J C A L I F O R N I A B
O A V G J W U F A L M U
U L E O O V E L F I U F
R E L X U N T S E F L F
W S X S R O S N T A E A
A D V E N T U R E M S L
G O N N E W M E X I C O
T R N E Y W E S J L Y T
P R A I R O J X L Y F F
```

California
New Mexico
prairie
wagons
buffalo
mules
family
travel
West
adventure
journey
trail

 _____

_____

 _____

_____

 _____

_____

 _____

_____

 _____

_____

 _____

_____

Name

# Did I Tell You About the Time I . . . ?

Do these suggestions give you any topic ideas?

a funny misunderstanding     getting a pet

a big decision     when I lost something

caught in a storm     learning something new

a scary experience     my moment of triumph

when I met someone important

## My Personal Narrative Topics   Write five experiences you have had that would make interesting stories.

**1** _____

**2** _____

**3** _____

**4** _____

**5** _____

Ask yourself these questions about each idea you wrote.

Can I remember
details about what
happened?

Would this interest
my audience?

Would I enjoy writing
about this?

Should I focus on
only one part of
this experience?

**Now circle the topic you want to write about.**

# Remembering the Details

Make a photo album for your narrative. Write your topic at the top of the page. Then draw "photos" of the important events in the order that they happened. List as many details as you can about what you saw, heard, smelled, touched, tasted, and how you felt.

_____

.........................................................................
Name

# Making It Better

Reread and revise your story, using the Revising Checklist. Then
use the Questions for a Writing Conference to help you discuss
your story with a classmate.

## Revising Checklist

☐ Does the beginning lead into the
story in an interesting way?

☐ Does this story describe the
experience the way I remember it?
Where should I add more details or
make them more vivid?

☐ Where can I use dialogue to bring
this experience to life?

☐ Did I tell how I felt?

## Questions for a Writing Conference

• What is good about this story?
• Does the beginning open the story in
an interesting way?
• Is the order of the events clear?
• Were any parts confusing?
• Where are more details or dialogue
needed to make the experience clearer?

Write notes to help you remember ideas discussed in your writing conference.

### My Notes

_____

_____

_____

_____

_____

_____

_____

_____

Name

# A Letter from the Wild West

Use the words in the box to complete the letter.

| | |
|---|---|
| culture | civilization |
| customs | traditional |
| primitive | myths |
| sacred | |

Dear Anne,

When I first left Chicago to move to Oregon, I thought I would never see

_____ again, but now I am getting used to it. We have seen

some Sioux. They seemed very _____ at first. Now, however, I

see that their _____ isn't better or worse than ours, it's just

different. They have their own _____ to explain the world around

them. They believe that buffalo are _____ and should only be

killed if necessary.

In spite of the differences, I have also seen some Sioux _____

that are similar to ours. Sioux children play some of the same games we do, and as they

grow up, boys and girls learn _____ tasks that their parents

have learned. Boys learn to hunt and ride, and girls help with cooking or caring for other

children. The more I learn about the Sioux people, the more I think we are more alike than

different.

Your friend,

Marie

**How might a Sioux child have described the settlers who moved onto
Sioux land during the days of the Wild West? Use three of the words
from the box to write a description on a separate sheet Cchof paper.**

Name

# Growing Up in the West

Complete the chart to show how relations between American
Indians and pioneers changed as more settlers moved to the West.
List three samples in each section. An example is provided for you.

| First Encounters | Many Settlers Arrive in the West | Late 1800s—Many Settlers in the West |
|---|---|---|
| most American Indians friendly | at first, small skirmishes | many American Indians forced to live on reservations |

List three things a Sioux boy did.

_____

_____

Which activity is most like something you do, and how?

_____

_____

# Understanding Judgments

Judgments are made based on knowledge and beliefs. Answer
the questions about the judgment used in the choices below.

**1** The young Sioux Ohiyesa shot a tiny arrow at a huge moose, even though he
knew he would not be able to kill it.

| What judgment did he make? | Why? |
|---|---|
| | |

**2** The American Indians made many treaties with the European settlers. Most of
these agreements were not honored by the newcomers.

| What judgment do you think the Indians made when making these treaties? | Why? |
|---|---|
| | |

**3** A Sioux chief referred to "a great equality" in men's and women's work.

| What judgment did the chief make about the value of work? | Why? |
|---|---|
| | |

**4** The European settlers often came into conflict with the Indians.

| What judgment did the settlers make? | Why? |
|---|---|
| | |

**5** You are an American Indian in 1850. A white settler appears at your camp.

| What do you think you would do? | Why? |
|---|---|
| | |

Name

# Step by Step

Use this chart to help plan your instructions. List each step, and give
details that your audience would need to know to do each step.

**MATERIALS**

| STEPS | DETAILS |
| --- | --- |
| STEP 1 | |
| STEP 2 | |
| STEP 3 | |
| STEP 4 | |
| STEP 5 | |

Name

# People Prefer Prefixes

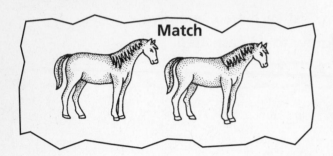

Match

Mismatch

Prefixes make a difference. In the letter spaces, write the word from the blanket that best completes each sentence. Then write the letters that appear in a triangle, circle, or box into their matching shapes. Unscramble the letters in the shapes to spell the names of three Native American groups.

disprove    disbelieve
exhale      exception
misplaced   misread
excuse      discourteous
mischief    misuse
displease

**1** His little sister is always getting into __ __ __ __ △ __ △ __ .

**2** People soon learn to __ __ __ ○ ○ __ __ __ __ a liar.

**3** I like all fruit with the __ □ __ __ __ __ □ □ __ of grapefruit.

**4** We looked all over for the __ __ __ △ __ △ △ __ __ key.

**5** It is __ __ __ __ __ ○ __ ○ __ __ __ __ to interrupt when someone is speaking.

**6** Write your name clearly so that I won't __ __ __ __ __ △ __ it.

**7** A fact is something you can't __ __ __ ○ __ ○ __ __ .

**8** She had a good __ __ __ □ □ __ for being late.

☐ → _____

○ → _____

△ → _____

Name

# Draw on Your Knowledge

Above each vocabulary word, draw the picture that appears beside the definition of that word.

**1**  stories that explain the beliefs of a people

**2** 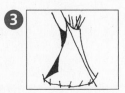 passed down from parents to children

**3**  a people's beliefs, ways of living, products, and laws; education, refinement

**4**  the everyday practices of a group of people

**5** 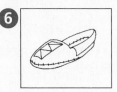 a kind of culture and society developed by a group of people

**6** 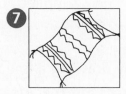 holy, deserving of great respect

**7** 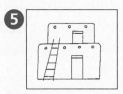 in an early stage of development

| | | | |
|---|---|---|---|
| | | | |
| **primitive** | **civilization** | **sacred** | **traditional** |

| | | |
|---|---|---|
| | | |
| **culture** | **customs** | **myths** |

On a separate sheet of paper, write three sentences that use two vocabulary words each.

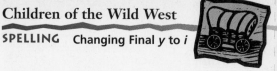

Name

# Tipi Match

**Changing Final *y* to *i*** Each Spelling Word is made up of an ending or a suffix added to a base word. Each base word ends with a consonant and *y*. If a word ends with a consonant and *y*, change the *y* to *i* when adding *-es*, *-ed*, *-er*, *-est*, or *-ness*.

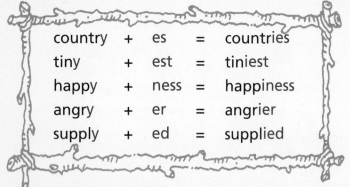

| country | + | es   | = | countries |
| tiny    | + | est  | = | tiniest   |
| happy   | + | ness | = | happiness |
| angry   | + | er   | = | angrier   |
| supply  | + | ed   | = | supplied  |

**My Study List**
What other words do you need to study for spelling? Add them to My Study List for *Children of the Wild West* in the back of this book.

**Form Spelling Words by drawing a line from the base word to the correct ending. Then cross out the letter in the base word that is replaced by *i* when the ending is added. Write each Spelling Word that you have formed.**

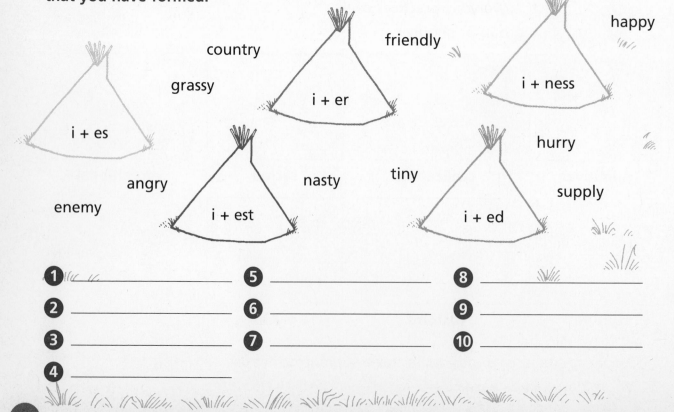

1. _____    5. _____    8. _____

2. _____    6. _____    9. _____

3. _____    7. _____    10. _____

4. _____

Name _____

# Spelling Spree

**Word Weave**  Use the clues to write the
Spelling Words that complete this puzzle.

**Spelling Words**
1. countries        6. enemies
2. supplied         7. tiniest
3. happiness        8. nastiest
4. hurried          9. grassier
5. angrier         10. friendliness

1 _ _ _ _ _ _ _           **1.** joy

2 _ _ _ _ _ _ _ _         **2.** opposite of kindest

3 _ _ _ _ _ _ _           **3.** smallest

4 _ _ _ _ _ _ _           **4.** rushed

5 _ _ _ _ _ _ _           **5.** opposite of friends

**Proofreading**  Find and circle five misspelled Spelling
Words in this song verse.  Then write each word correctly.

Once we wandered grasier prairies,

Life supplied by buffalo.

Then came changes, agrier faces —

Say good-bye to all we know.

    Days of plenty, evening frendliness,

    Lights from campfires shone on happiness.

Different sights now, strange new countrees,

    Puzzled by life's changing show,

Say good-bye to all we know,

Say farewell to all we know.

6  _____

7 _____

8 _____

9  _____

10 _____

**A Day in the Life**  Imagine you are a Kiowa, Comanche, or
Navajo child in the 1800s. On a separate sheet of paper, write a diary
entry that tells what your day would be like. What chores did you do?
How did you spend your spare time? Use Spelling Words from the list.

# Game Day

**Subject and Object Pronouns** Finish your journal entry about yesterday's game day by writing the correct pronouns. Above each one write **S** for subject pronoun or **O** for object pronoun. Then write a final sentence, using a subject pronoun or an object pronoun.

Subject Pronouns
I           we
you         you
she, he, it  they

Object Pronouns
me          us
you         you
her, him, it  them

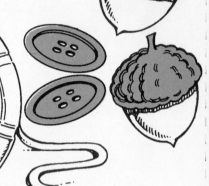

Example:  **We** had a wonderful time yesterday!
          (We, Us)

_____ went with several friends to game day in the village. First,
(I, me)

_____ watched the breath-holding contest with Yancy and Nita.
(we, us)

_____ offered the prize to _____. Then _____ won
(He, Him)                    (she, her)              (they, them)

the three-legged race as we cheered _____ on. Later a girl
                                    (they, them)

showed yo-yo tricks to my brother and _____. Then _____
                                      (I, me)            (she, her)

gave a yo-yo to _____. Next, Yancy and _____ joined a
                (we, us)                        (he, him)

game of blindman's bluff. At the end of the day, Yancy and _____
                                                            (I, me)

rode horses. Horseback riding was the most fun for _____.
                                                   (he, him)

_____

_____

Name _____

# Heading West

## Subject and Object Pronouns
Help Sam correct his letter. If a sentence contains an unnecessary double subject (a noun subject followed by a subject pronoun), use the delete sign ( ✐ ) to cross out one. Write subject or object pronouns above the underlined words.

**Example:** This letter i̶s̶ i̶s̶ for my friend Kenji, and I want to mail

       **it**        **him**

this letter to Kenji soon.

---

Dear Kenji,

My mom she is planning a trip to the Great Plains. My family and

I are looking forward to the trip. Because the Great Plains are vast

and level, the Great Plains are great for riding horses. By the time

a Native American boy was five or six, a boy might have a horse.

Many Native Americans rode bareback. I want to ride like the

Native Americans. My dad he said I might try riding bareback at

my grandparents' house. My grandparents have two horses for my

family and me. Riding bareback is hard, but I'm not scared to try

riding bareback. María she says I'll probably fall off the horse.

Sam'll show María that María is wrong! _____

_____.

                                      Sincerely,

                                      Sam

**Write a closing line for the letter. Use a subject pronoun
and an object pronoun.**

Pecos Bill
SELECTION VOCABULARY

# A Western Scene

Label the picture, using the correct words from the box.

| homestead | stagecoaches | cowpoke |
|-----------|--------------|---------|
| hootenanny | coyotes | |

Write a paragraph describing the picture.
Use all five vocabulary words.

_____

_____

_____

_____

_____

_____

_____

_____

_____

Copyright © Houghton Mifflin Company. All rights reserved.

198   From the Prairie to the Sea

# Put It Together

After reading *Pecos Bill*, complete the sentence on each puzzle piece. Then number the pieces 1 through 10, based on the order of the events in the story. Cut the pieces out and put them together, following the numbers. When you are finished, your puzzle will look like Pecos Bill's home state!

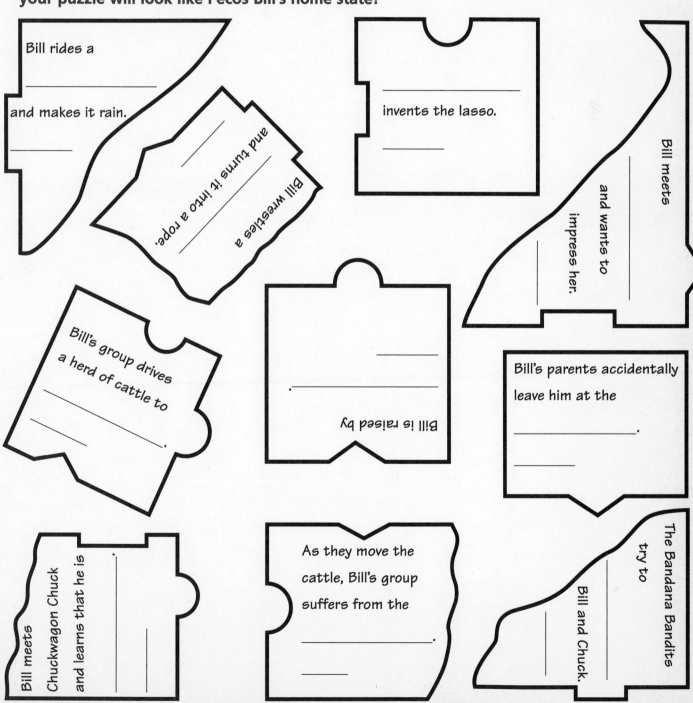

Bill rides a

_____

and makes it rain.

_____

Bill wrestles a

_____

and turns it into a rope.

_____

invents the lasso.

_____

Bill meets

_____

and wants to impress her.

_____

Bill's group drives a herd of cattle to

_____

_____

_____

Bill is raised by

_____

Bill's parents accidentally leave him at the

_____

_____

Bill meets Chuckwagon Chuck and learns that he is

_____

_____

As they move the cattle, Bill's group suffers from the

_____

_____

The Bandana Bandits try to

_____

Bill and Chuck.

# How Great-Grandmother Dusted Texas

**Read the tale. Use it to write simple directions for how to dust Texas. You can number the steps or use order words to show the sequence. Hint: There are seven steps.**

Great-grandmother told me that when she was just a tiny cowgirl, she dusted the whole state of Texas.

One dry Texas spring, a powerful dust storm left knee-deep dust over all of Texas. Great-grandmother wanted to get rid of the dust, but how? She decided to hold a hootenanny.

Great-grandmother then built a huge dance floor. The singers and fiddlers began singing and playing, and the dancers began to turn and twirl. It was such fun that soon all of Texas joined in. All that singing and twirling set off a whirlwind. Great-grandmother caught the whirlwind in her sunbonnet and dragged it to the mouth of the Rio Grande River. She held the tip of the whirlwind down where the Rio Grande emptied into the Gulf of Mexico until every speck of dust in Texas landed there. The river and the gulf were so wet that the dust soaked up the water and settled down to form the muddy delta of the Rio Grande, which is still there today.

## How to Dust Texas

_____

_____

_____

_____

_____

_____

_____

_____

Name

# Cactus Caper

**Read about Pecos Bill and the fast-talkin', low-down, cactus-rustlin' Texas Ted. Rewrite the paragraph into a scene for a play. Include stage directions in parentheses. Give your other characters appropriate cowboy names!**

Texas Ted's helpers are loading cactus plants into a covered wagon. Texas Ted is shouting orders and threats at them, and they are complaining about the hard work. Pecos Bill spots Texas Ted. Bill's men suggest different ways to surprise and capture Texas Ted, but Bill has his own idea. He silences them and begins to describe his plan.

# On Stage

**Tale of a Contraction**

The cow's mooing loudly.

Your school is going to stage *Pecos Bill*. You've taken notes
at a meeting about props and special effects. Rewrite your
notes without using a contraction or a possessive. Then
organize your notes by writing **P** for possessive
or **C** for contraction in each box.

*Props Manager*

*Can-Do Special Effects Team*

**1** Bill's fishing pole is broken.

_____

**2** We've found a drum for the thunder.

_____

**3** Chuck's spurs jangle.

_____

**4** You'll make it rain, right?

_____

**5** We don't need to see the tornado; let's hear it!

_____

**6** The bandits' bandanas are dirty.

_____

**7** The cactus's suitcase is full.

_____

**8** Sue's "Miss Kansas" sash is pretty.

_____

**9** We can't use live coyotes; create sound effects.

_____

Name

# Create a Cowboy Tale

In small groups, create a story using the numbered words. Begin by telling the group the definition of the word *homestead.* Then write the first sentence of a tall tale using *homestead,* and read it to the group. Then provide a synonym or a definition for *round up* and write a sentence using that phrase that continues the tale. Continue until all the numbered words have been defined and used in the story. Have a volunteer read the story to the class.

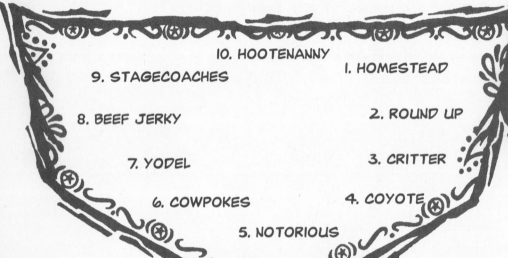

10. HOOTENANNY

9. STAGECOACHES

8. BEEF JERKY

7. YODEL

6. COWPOKES

5. NOTORIOUS

1. HOMESTEAD

2. ROUND UP

3. CRITTER

4. COYOTE

_____

_____

_____

_____

_____

_____

_____

_____

_____

_____

Name

# Loopy Lasso Action

**Adding -ion** Each pair of Spelling Words is made up of a verb and a noun. The verb in each pair is the base word. The noun is formed by adding the suffix *-ion* to the verb. When a verb ends with **e**, drop the **e** before adding *-ion*.

**Verb:**    act         create
**Noun:**    action      creation

Write the verb form of a Spelling Word that fits each clue. Then add the suffix *-ion* and write the noun form of the Spelling Word.

## CLUES

**1–2** to perform; to behave

**3–4** to instruct or order

**5–6** to own; to have as a quality

**7–8** to produce; to make

**9–10** to tell; to read aloud

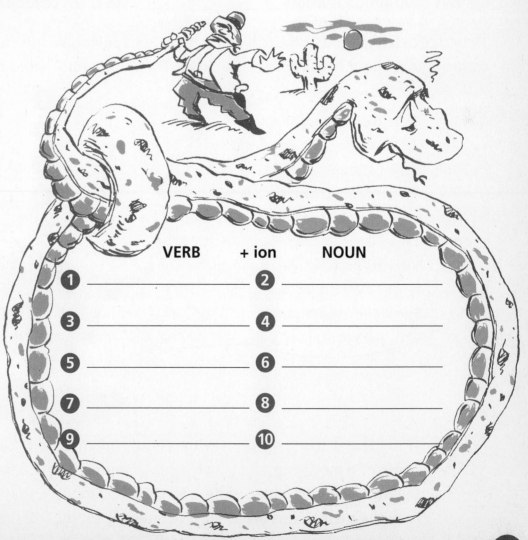

VERB   + ion   NOUN

1 _____  2 _____
3 _____  4 _____
5 _____  6 _____
7 _____  8 _____
9 _____  10 _____

........................................................
Name

# Spelling Spree

**Tongue Twisters** Write a Spelling Word to complete Pecos Bill's favorite tongue twisters.

**1** Does Atoka Al _____ like an

Arapaho or an Apache?

**2** Nevada Ned never knew that _____ was needed for

the Natchez News.

**3** Please pack each _____ in your poncho, Panhandle Pete.

**4** Why does Navajo Nell _____ nearly every new announcement?

**5** This contraption is a cute _____ to catch coyotes!

**Proofreading** Find and circle five misspelled Spelling Words in this traffic report about Pecos Bill's cattle drive. Then write each word correctly.

We're seeing plenty of acton on the trails today as longhorns move in the direcion of the stockyards. The cattle are clogging all major routes into town. Since cattle posess no understanding of traffic laws, they'll creat huge jams downtown for the next two hours. Should any cattle stroll onto your land, please stay calm but act quickly. Just derect the nearest cowpoke to the stray cow.

**6** _____

**7** _____

**8** _____

**9** _____

**10** _____

**It's Like This** Legends say that Pecos Bill invented the cattle drive. Think of a modern gadget such as the computer or laser scanner. On a separate sheet of paper, write a truth-stretching tale that explains how the gadget was invented. Use Spelling Words from the list.

# Whose Cow?

## Possessive Pronouns

The cattle drive is over, and the
cows have been auctioned off.
Help the auctioneer find each
buyer's cow. Complete each
sentence with a different
possessive pronoun. Write your
own sentences for the pictures.

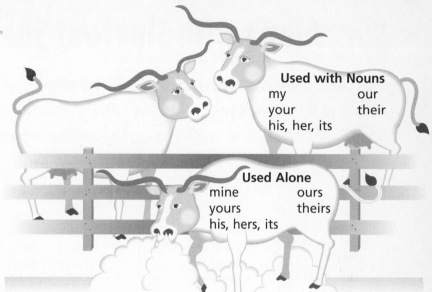

**Used with Nouns**
my                          our
your                       their
his, her, its

**Used Alone**
mine                      ours
yours                     theirs
his, hers, its

**Examples:** Your cow has very short horns. The cow with

very short horns is yours.

**1** _____ cow has very long horns.

**2** _____ cow is drinking water.

**3** _____ cow is eating hay.

**4** _____

_____

**5** _____

_____

**6** The cow with long horns is _____

**7** The cow drinking water is _____

**8** _____

_____

**9** _____

_____

**10** _____

_____

# Sing Along with Sluefoot Sue

## Possessive Pronouns and Contractions with Pronouns

**Help Sue finish her song. Write the correct contraction over each pair of
underlined words and write the correct possessive pronoun in the blank.**

| Possessive Pronouns | Contractions |
|---|---|
| its | it's (it is, it has) |
| your | you're (you are) |
| his | he's (he is, he has) |
| their | they're (they are) |
| theirs | there's (there is) |

<u>I will</u> sing you _____ (my, mine) song; <u>it is</u> about Pecos Bill.

Out here in _____ (our, ours) state <u>we are</u> amazed by him still.

He tamed a tornado with _____ (his, he's) rope made of snake

And gave cows to Kansas, where <u>they are</u> now eating steak.

**(Refrain)**

<u>He has</u> been raised by coyotes!

<u>You have</u> just got to know <u>he is</u>

The wiliest, smiliest, consarndest, gosh-darndest coyote kid in the West!

He invented the lasso, the roundup as well.

<u>He has</u> invented the yodel—taught the cowpokes _____

(they're, their) yell.

And if <u>you had</u> seen a cowpoke before Bill came through,

<u>You would</u> be right in believing <u>he had</u> improved on them, too.

**(Refrain)**

Name _____

# Planning a TV Commercial

Imagine that Captain Aubry of *Along the Santa Fe Trail* could advertise his wagon train on television. Plan a TV commercial for him. Use the chart to help you plan.

| | |
|---|---|
| Reread the beginning of *Along the Santa Fe Trail*. What hardships did pioneers face? | |
| What help could a leader such as Captain Aubry offer? | |
| What propaganda techniques could you use to persuade people to travel with Captain Aubry? | |

**Plan the pictures and script.**

| Pictures | | | |
|---|---|---|---|
| Script | | | |

On another sheet of paper, make a final copy of your plan. Use it to present your plan to your group or class. Check the list to see that your work is complete.

## Revising Checklist

☐ My work reflects the hardships described in *Along the Santa Fe Trail*.
☐ I've made good judgments about how Captain Aubry can help travelers.
☐ I can explain at least two propaganda techniques I have used.

Name

# Do You *Believe* This??

What "unbelievable" event happens in each selection? Fill out each column in the chart as you complete the selections in the theme.

| | La Bamba | Willie Bea and the Time the Martians Landed |
|---|---|---|
| What is the genre of the selection? | | |
| What surprising or unexpected event does the selection tell about? | | |
| What causes this event to happen? | | |
| How do people react to this event? | | |

What have you learned in this theme about how realistic and fantastic events can combine in what you read? _____

_____

_____

Name

# Do You *Believe* This??

What "unbelievable" event happens in each selection? Fill out each
column in the chart as you complete the selections in the theme.

|  | McBroom Tells the Truth | Trapped in Tar |
|---|---|---|
| **What is the genre of the selection?** |  |  |
| **What surprising or unexpected event does the selection tell about?** |  |  |
| **What causes this event to happen?** |  |  |
| **How do people react to this event?** |  |  |

Tell about a time in your own life when reality seemed hard to believe. _____

_____

_____

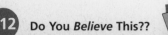

Name _____

# A Golden Oldie

**Use the vocabulary words to complete the sentences. Then answer the questions.**

forty-five record

talent

limelight

Wilky and Wally

duo

debut

pantomime

Hey, Dad, I just got this

_____.

It's by a _____

called Willy and Wally. I think

it's their first record, their

_____,

so it might be valuable.

Willy and Wally? I remember them!

We used to _____ the

words to their music! They had so much

_____. They were in the

_____ for years!

**1** What would you do in a talent show? _____

**2** How would you feel if you were making your debut as a performer? _____

_____

**3** What would you do to pantomime a song? _____

_____

**4** How would it feel to be in the limelight? _____

_____

Name

# Talent Scout's Report

Complete the talent scout's report about the main character and the events in "La Bamba."

John Burroughs Elementary Talent Show

Admit One

**1** Performer's first name and talent: _____

_____

**2** Unusual events during the performance: _____

_____

_____

**3** Audience reaction during the performance: _____

_____

_____

_____

**4** Performer's previous experience in front of an audience: _____

_____

_____

**5** Performer's prospects for a future in show business: _____

_____

_____

Do You *Believe* This??

Name

# Sum It Up

Write a summary of "La Bamba" for a book jacket. Think about the story elements on the index card. Then write your summary using complete sentences.

The story is about _____

_____

_____

_____

_____

_____

_____

_____

_____

_____

_____

_____

_____

_____

**Story Structure**
Main character
Setting
Problem
Three events
Resolution

Do You *Believe* This?? 215

# Who's on First?

These photographs were taken during a
school talent show. Write a caption for each.
Include at least one pronoun in each caption.

1 _____

_____

_____

2 _____

_____

_____

3 _____

_____

_____

_____

4 _____

_____

_____

5 _____

_____

_____

_____

Name

# The Spotlight's on You!

All the words in the spotlights begin with the prefix *con-* or one of its forms (*col-, com-*). Find the word that matches each clue and write it in the letter spaces. Then read the tinted letters down to find out what every performer wants.

converge

collide

The prefix *con-* (or *com-* or *col-*) means "together" or "with."

collection
contract
compound

compatible
compete
collapse
compare
companion

**1** a written agreement ＿ ＿ ＿ ＿ ＿ ＿ ＿ ＿

**2** able to live together in harmony ＿ ＿ ＿ ＿ ＿ ＿ ＿ ＿ ＿ ＿

**3** to look for likenesses ＿ ＿ ＿ ＿ ＿ ＿ ＿

**4** a group of stamps, for instance ＿ ＿ ＿ ＿ ＿ ＿ ＿ ＿ ＿ ＿

**5** someone to go places with ＿ ＿ ＿ ＿ ＿ ＿ ＿ ＿ ＿

**6** word made up of two or more other words ＿ ＿ ＿ ＿ ＿ ＿ ＿ ＿

**7** what a waterlogged tent might do ＿ ＿ ＿ ＿ ＿ ＿ ＿ ＿

**8** what athletes do ＿ ＿ ＿ ＿ ＿ ＿ ＿

Write two sentences about "La Bamba," using a word from the spotlight in each.

＿＿＿＿＿＿＿＿＿＿＿＿＿＿＿＿＿＿＿＿＿＿＿＿＿＿＿＿＿＿

＿＿＿＿＿＿＿＿＿＿＿＿＿＿＿＿＿＿＿＿＿＿＿＿＿＿＿＿＿＿

Do You *Believe* This??

Name

# Preview a Performance

You are writing a preview of the school talent show for the school newspaper. Use the words on the curtains in your article about the scene shown.

limelight

pantomime

talent

debut

duo

forty-five record

rehearsal

slapstick

melodramatic

wings

# Song Sort

**Name**

## The Prefixes *in-* and *con-*

Each Spelling Word is made up of the prefix *in-*, *im-*, *con-*, or *com-* and a base word or word root. A **prefix** is a word part added to the beginning of a base word or a word root. A prefix adds meaning to the word. A **word root** is a word part that has meaning, but unlike a base word, a word root usually cannot stand alone.

To spell a word with a prefix, think of the prefix and then the base word or the word root. Spell the word using its parts.

### Spelling Words

1. impress
2. confuse
3. conduct
4. inhale
5. intent
6. command
7. immediate
8. compete
9. impolite
10. connect

**My Study List**
What other words do you need to study for spelling? Add them to My Study List for "La Bamba" in the back of this book.

| Prefix | Meaning | Word | Meaning |
|--------|---------|------|---------|
| in-, im- | in; toward; not; without | inhale | to breathe in |
|  |  | impolite | not polite |
| con-, com- | together; with | confuse | to mix up with |
|  |  | compete | to strive together or with |

**Write each Spelling Word on the record with the matching prefix.**

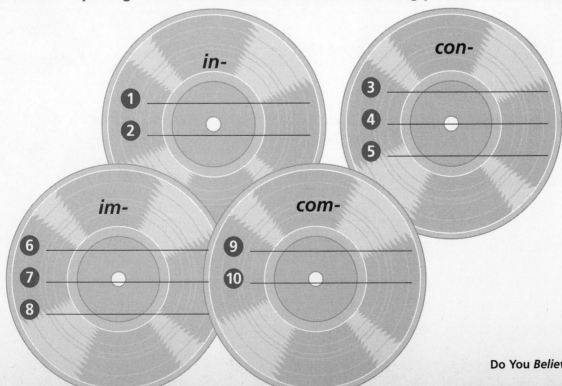

*in-*

1. _____
2. _____

*con-*

3. _____
4. _____
5. _____

*im-*

6. _____
7. _____
8. _____

*com-*

9. _____
10. _____

Name _____

# Spelling Spree

**Proofreading** **Find and circle four misspelled Spelling Words in this school announcement. Then write each word correctly.**

Do you sing or cunduct a band? Can you comand a dog to jump through a hoop? Would you like to conpete in a yodeling contest? If so, sign up today! Make imediate plans to be part of our Spring Talent Show. Have fun and impress your friends and family!!

**1** _____     **3** _____

**2** _____     **4** _____

## Word Trios **Write the Spelling Word that goes with each group.**

**5** rude, thoughtless, _____

**6** bewilder, muddle, _____

**7** affect, influence, _____

**8** determined, firm, _____

**9** join, link, _____

**10** breathe, sniff, _____

**Now Starring** Imagine that you've been asked to perform in the school talent show. On a separate sheet of paper, write a short song that you could sing, perhaps to familiar music. Use Spelling Words from the list.

# Talent Tryout

**Double Negatives** Read the poster. Use the proofreaders' delete mark ( ) to remove double negatives.

I haven't never been in a talent show.

I haven't never been in a talent show.

**Do not use double negatives in a sentence.**

You haven't never been in a talent show like this! Imagine yourself on a dark stage. The audience isn't not making a sound. They are waiting for your brilliant performance. Suddenly, the lights shine. The crowd gasps. Nobody hasn't seen a costume like yours before. You couldn't never have a better time. So sign up to be in the show. Don't hide your talents—share them with the world. For more information, come to room 315 after school on Friday. You haven't got nothing to lose. You might even win!

Write a paragraph about your act. Your paragraph should have at least five sentences and use three negative words.

_____

_____

_____

_____

_____

_____

Name

# Record Breakers

**Double Negatives**  Manuel could use a rule book on caring
for records. Use the negative word next to each picture to write
the rule that goes with each picture.

**Example:** Do not touch the grooves.     *not*

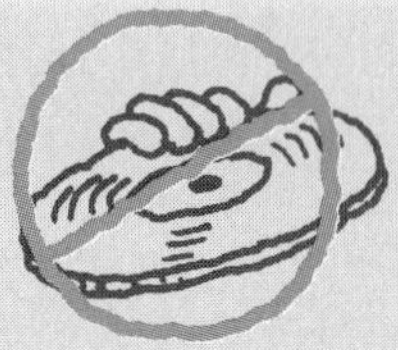

*never*   **1** _____

_____

*not*   **2** _____

_____

*not*   **3** _____

_____

*never*   **4** _____

_____

*nothing*   **5** _____

_____

*never*   **6** _____

_____

**More!**  On a separate sheet of paper, write four rules about
caring for a cassette tape or CD. Use a negative word in each rule.

Name _____

# Martian Mania!

Read each definition in the jack-o'-lantern. Then write the
matching vocabulary word in each shape.

alien
Martians
Venus
universe
outlandish

1. second planet from the sun

**1**

2. bizarre; strange

**2**

**3**

3. a being from outer space

4. Earth, the galaxies, and space

**4**

5. beings from Mars

**5**

Use each vocabulary word in a sentence.

**6** _____

**7** _____

**8** _____

**9** _____

**10** _____

# What Really Happened?

Read each statement about *Willie Bea
and the Time the Martians Landed.*
Check **T** if it's true or **F** if it's false. Then
answer the question.

**T    F**

**1** Willie Bea and Toughy Clay have heard on TV that aliens have
landed.  ___  ___

**2** Willie Bea has been invited to a costume party at the Kelly farm.  ___  ___

**3** Toughy Clay has never been on the Kelly road before.  ___  ___

**4** Willie Bea believes that beings from Venus have landed.  ___  ___

**5** The children mistake a shooting star for an alien spaceship.  ___  ___

**6** They both hear a loud rumbling they can't identify.  ___  ___

**7** Toughy Clay explains that the shapes they see are really farm
machines.  ___  ___

**8** Willie Bea tries to escape and falls off her stilts.  ___  ___

**9** Willie Bea mistakes a person's voice for an alien's.  ___  ___

**10** The "aliens" turn out to be automobiles.  ___  ___

What really happened to the children in the story?

_____

_____

_____

_____

_____

_____

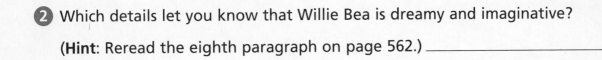

# What Did *You* Notice?

Write your answers to the questions. The hints are there to help you.

**1** What did the Kelly house look like? (**Hint**: Reread the third paragraph on page 561.) _____

_____

**2** Which details let you know that Willie Bea is dreamy and imaginative? (**Hint**: Reread the eighth paragraph on page 562.) _____

_____

**3** Which detail lets you know Toughy is nervous when Willie Bea asks him where he saw the monster? (**Hint**: Reread the last paragraph on page 562.)

_____

_____

**4** What did Willie Bea see that made her "transfixed by the monsters"? (**Hint**: Reread the fourth paragraph on page 567.) _____

_____

_____

Now use the details from the selection to draw a picture of one of the monsters Willie Bea thought she saw.

Do You *Believe* This??  225

Name

# Along the Winding Road

Each picture shows the same scene from a different point of view.
Write three sentences under each one, describing what you see.
Use adjectives and adverbs to describe the pictures clearly.

1 _____

_____

2 _____

_____

3 _____

_____

4 _____

_____

5 _____

_____

6 _____

_____

Do You *Believe* This??

Name
_____

# Impossible Puzzle?

Write the word that matches each clue. (Use the code after each clue to help you.) Then write the numbered letters to solve the puzzle.

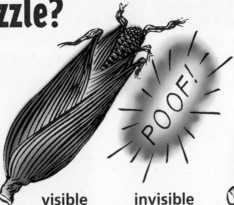

visible    invisible

**The prefix *in-* means "not."**

exterior    interior

**The prefix *in-* means "within or into."**

| CODE Forms of the Prefix *in-* | | | |
|---|---|---|---|
| N | L | R | M |
| *in-* | *il-* | *ir-* | *im-* |

**1** not able to get a disease   **CODE M**

___ ___ ___ ___ ___ ___ ___
       14  12

**2** not perfect   **CODE M**

___ ___ ___ ___ ___ ___ ___ ___ ___
          5              10

**3** not able to read   **CODE L**

___ ___ ___ ___ ___ ___ ___ ___ ___
    8                  3   2   7

**4** to take air into the lungs   **CODE N**

___ ___ ___ ___ ___ ___
          1           16

**5** not dependable   **CODE R**

___ ___ ___ ___ ___ ___ ___ ___ ___ ___ ___ ___ ___ ___
       17        11  15   6       13

**6** not handy   **CODE N**

___ ___ ___ ___ ___ ___ ___ ___ ___ ___
              4       9

irresponsible, environment, illiterate, immune, enclose, illegible, enforce, imperfect, inconvenient, envelope, encircle, illustrate, inhale

What Willie Bea really saw:

___ ___ ___ ___ ___ ___ ___ ___ ___   g   ___ ___ ___ ___ ___ ___ ___
 1   2   3   4   5   6   7   8   9      10  11  12  13  14  15  16  17

On another sheet of paper, write two sentences about the story. In each sentence, use a word with a form of the prefix *in-*.

Do You *Believe* This??   **227**

Name

# A Strange and Starry Night

Write each vocabulary word next to its
definition. Then if you see the number 1,
circle the first letter of the vocabulary
word. If you see the number 2, circle
the second letter, and so forth.

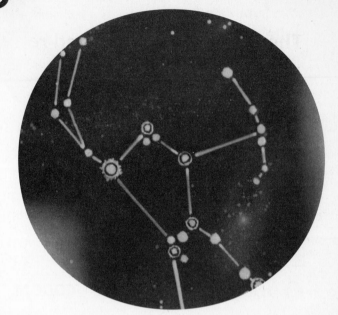

| | |
|---|---|
| alien | Martians |
| bizarre | monstrous |
| celestial | outlandish |
| cosmos | universe |
| fantastic | Venus |

(2, 8)  beings from the planet Mars _____

(2)  a being from another planet  _____

(5)  the second planet from the sun _____

(1, 3)  unfamiliar and very strange _____

(2)  everything that exists _____

(3, 4)  unbelievable; existing only in imagination _____

(7)  very strange or odd _____

(2)  exceptionally large; scary-looking _____

(3, 7)  having to do with the sky _____

(1)  the orderly system of everything that exists _____

Unscramble the letters you circled to complete the sentence.

If Willie Bea had looked at the stars, she might have seen Orion and other

___ ___ ___ ___ ___ ___ ___ ___ ___ ___ ___ ___ ___ ___.

Name _____

# Word Combine

**The Prefixes *un-*, *dis-*, and *re-***  Each Spelling Word has the prefix **un-**, **dis-**, or **re-**. To spell a word with a prefix, think of the prefix and then the base word or the word root. Spell the word using its parts.

| Prefix | Meaning |
|--------|---------|
| un- | not; opposite |
| dis- | apart; opposite |
| re- | again; back |

| Word | Meaning |
|------|---------|
| unclear | not clear |
| distant | standing apart; far off |
| remove | to take back or away |

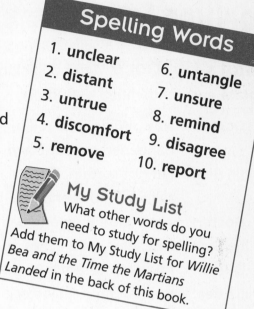

## Spelling Words

1. unclear
2. distant
3. untrue
4. discomfort
5. remove
6. untangle
7. unsure
8. remind
9. disagree
10. report

My Study List
What other words do you need to study for spelling? Add them to My Study List for *Willie Bea and the Time the Martians Landed* in the back of this book.

Make Spelling Words by adding the correct prefix to each base word or word root. Then write the Spelling Words.

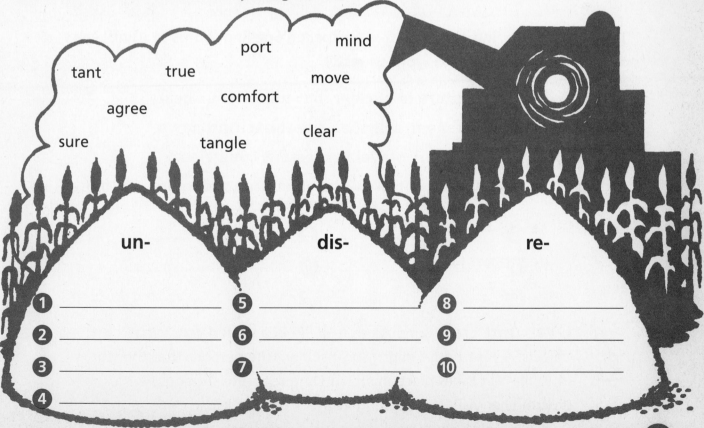

tant   true   port   mind
agree   comfort   move
sure   tangle   clear

**un-**
1 _____
2 _____
3 _____
4 _____

**dis-**
5 _____
6 _____
7 _____

**re-**
8 _____
9 _____
10 _____

Name

# Spelling Spree

## What's Up, Doc? Write a Spelling Word to replace each underlined definition.

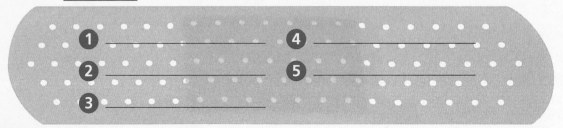

**Spelling Words**

1. unclear
2. distant
3. untrue
4. discomfort
5. remove
6. untangle
7. unsure
8. remind
9. disagree
10. report

**Doctor:** Now, Willie Bea, tell me what happened in that cornfield.

**Willie Bea:** I'm <u>not certain</u>, Doctor. I remember falling. And then some farmers helped me <u>take off</u> my stilts.

**Doctor:** Are you feeling any pain?

**Willie Bea:** Just some <u>mild aches</u>, but I'm sure it's nothing serious.

**Doctor:** I <u>think differently.</u> You may have broken a bone.

**Willie Bea:** Wait a minute, Doctor! That light on your forehead does <u>help me to remember</u> about something! I saw Martians last night!

1. _____    4. _____

2. _____    5. _____

3. _____

## Proofreading Find and circle five misspelled Spelling Words in Aunt Leah's predictions. Then write each word correctly.

* Your future is uncleer, but follow your heart. *

* A stranger will soon riport exciting news.*

* You will travel to disstant countries.*

* Never tell unntrue tales, for then you must untangel more and more lies. *

6. _____    9. _____

7. _____    10. _____

8. _____

## Over and Out Suppose that Willie Bea visited you. What objects in your house might surprise her? (Remember that the story of Willie Bea takes place in 1938.) On a separate sheet of paper, describe her visit. Use Spelling Words from the list.

Name _____

# Never Did a Night Last Longer . . .

**Adverbs** Toughy has already drawn pictures in his journal about the scary night. Help him complete his story. Write adverbs that tell *how*, *when*, or *where*. Then draw a final picture for the journal, and write a sentence using an adverb.

**When**

first          then
later         next
second      today
often        yesterday

**Where**

there          somewhere
outside       elsewhere
forward

**How**

fast          quickly
nervously    gently
happily      suddenly
            eerily

The sun sets _____ (when) in the fall. Willie Bea and I _____ (how) put on our costumes. We walked _____ (how) on our stilts. The moon shone _____ (how) over the fields, and the corn swayed _____ (how) in the night breeze. _____ (where) is the farmer who tried to stop us. The Kellys were having a party _____ (where) two combines were _____ (when) harvesting the corn. _____ (when) we saw a strange light! Willie Bea tried _____ (how) to get away.

_____

_____

_____

_____

Name

# The Kelly Party

My light shines brightly.
I hold it tight.

My light shines **more** brightly.
I hold it tight**er** than before.

My light shines **most** brightly.
I hold it tight**est** of all.

## Comparing with Adverbs Write a summary of the party at the Kelly farm. Write five sentences using adverbs, comparing the actions of the people shown in the picture. Use adverbs from the box if you wish.

| soon |
| sooner |
| soonest |
| fiercely |
| more fiercely |
| most fiercely |
| fast |
| faster |
| fastest |
| hungrily |
| more hungrily |
| most hungrily |
| often |
| more often |
| most often |
| noisily |
| more noisily |
| most noisily |

Name

# Put It in Writing

Write the correct vocabulary word on the line
above each caption. Then write four sentences of
your own, each using a different vocabulary word.

| | |
|---|---|
| foreclose | bargain |
| deed | profit |
| legal | loophole |

_____

This officially allows
Tim to own Tom's
tree house.

_____

Larry sells a bushel
of corn but has to pay
Mary for the seeds.
This is the money he
has left over.

_____

Hester agrees to
wash the dishes, and
Chester agrees to dry
them. This is what
they've made.

_____

If Peter doesn't pay
her by next week,
Polly will do this by
taking back the bicycle
he is buying from her.

_____

This part of the
agreement says that
Will can't own Jill's
pogo stick if he can't
ride it in a week.

_____

Little Clarinda says
that if things aren't
done according to the
law, they're not this.

1 _____

_____

2 _____

_____

3 _____

_____

4 _____

_____

Name

# Who's Who and What's What?

Write the correct answers from the choices in the box.

1. Who has the worst farmland in Iowa? _____

2. Who figures out how to find three moths in the daytime? _____

3. Who has pumpkin races on the farm? _____

4. Who spits out watermelon seeds on the McBrooms' farm? _____

5. Who tries to entertain Hector Jones as he rides with the McBrooms to their

   new farm? _____

Write the answer to each question.

6. What is the first trick that Hector Jones plays on the McBrooms? _____

   _____

7. What does McBroom have in his purse besides a ten-dollar bill? _____

   _____

8. What event turns the pond into good farming land? _____

   _____

9. What is the last trick that Hector Jones plays on the McBrooms? _____

   _____

10. What does Josh McBroom finally do to get rid of Hector Jones? _____

    _____

# Make It Real–or Fantasy!

**Read the sentence starters. If the sentence is labeled F, add the ending that makes the sentence a fantasy. If it is labeled R, add the ending that makes the sentence realistic. Then write a fantasy sentence and a realistic sentence of your own.**

**1** **R** The McBroom family traveled to Iowa in _____.
an automobile / a vacuum cleaner

**2** **R** They counted noses and found that _____.
Larry was being counted twice / Larry had too many noses

**3** **F** Heck Jones sold them a farm that turned out to be _____.
a one-acre pond / a giant iceberg

**4** **F** The water in the pond _____.
evaporated in a sudden dry spell / was deep and muddy

**5** **R** When McBroom planted seeds, _____.
he planted them three inches apart / they grew instantly

**6** **F** Heck Jones insisted that Josh McBroom owed him _____.
three white moths / a unicorn

**7** **R** The McBroom children learned to ride _____.
corn stalks / bicycles

**8** **F** Heck Jones went flying home _____.
in an airplane / on a banana squash

**9** **F** _____

_____

**10** **R** _____

_____

_____

Name

# The Beanstalk and Jack

**Read each sentence. Decide if the underlined word or group of words can be moved to another part of the sentence. If yes, rewrite the sentence, moving the word or words. If no, explain why not.**

**1** Jack planted the magical seed <u>in the ground.</u>

_____

_____

**2** A beanstalk began to grow <u>within seconds</u>!

_____

_____

**3** Jack watched the beanstalk shoot up <u>above the rooftops</u>.

_____

_____

**4** Jack climbed the beanstalk <u>rapidly</u>.

_____

_____

**5** Jack saw a sleeping giant <u>when he reached the top</u>.

_____

_____

# Automatic Fun!

Fill in the crossword puzzle. If the clue contains the word part *self*, use a word with the word root *auto*. If the clue contains a form of the word *write* or *record*, use a word with the word root *graph*.

I wrote it...

...my<u>self</u>!

All About Me: An <u>Auto</u>biography

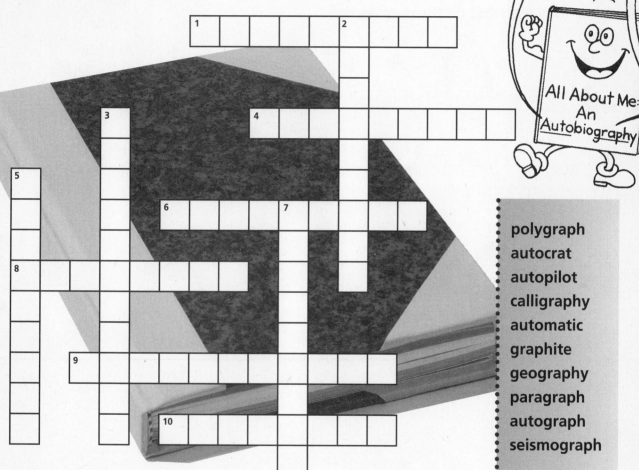

polygraph
autocrat
autopilot
calligraphy
automatic
graphite
geography
paragraph
autograph
seismograph

**Across**

1. operating by itself
4. mechanism to let a vehicle steer itself
6. recorder of someone's truths or lies
8. a ruler who keeps all the power to himself or herself
9. fancy writing
10. the part of a pencil that writes

**Down**

2. your name when you write it yourself
3. recorder of earthquake signs
5. a way of organizing writing
7. study of the earth; writing about the earth

Name

# Pick a Pair of Pumpkins

In the box, you will find five pairs of synonyms and one word that stands alone. Write the pairs of synonyms on the pumpkins by the pairs of children. Write the remaining word on little Clarinda's pumpkin. On a separate sheet of paper, write a sentence for each word on the pumpkins.

- deed
- escape clause
- evict
- legal
- profit
- lawful
- contract
- loophole
- bargain
- gain
- foreclose

# Suffix Patch

**Words with Suffixes** Each Spelling Word contains the suffix *-ly*, *-ful*, *-ness*, *-less*, or *-ment*. A **suffix** is a word part added to the end of a base word. A suffix adds meaning to the word. The spelling of a base word is usually not changed when the suffix begins with a consonant.

| Suffix | Meaning | Word |
|--------|---------|------|
| -ly | in a certain way | exact**ly** |
| -ful | full of | wonder**ful** |
| -ness | the condition or quality of | kind**ness** |
| -less | without | count**less** |
| -ment | the condition of | excite**ment** |

## Spelling Words

1. wonderful
2. countless
3. excitement
4. exactly
5. kindness
6. sleepless
7. mouthful
8. brightness
9. finally
10. government

**My Study List**
What other words do you need to study for spelling? Add them to My Study List for *McBroom Tells the Truth* in the back of this book.

**Write each Spelling Word on the watermelon with the matching suffix.**

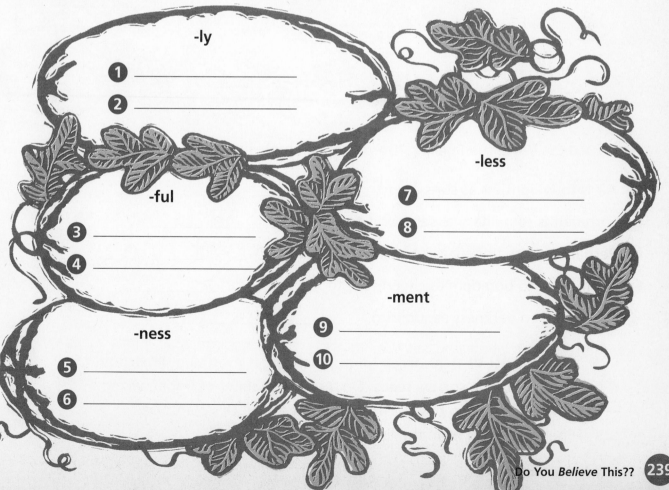

-ly
1 _____
2 _____

-ful
3 _____
4 _____

-ness
5 _____
6 _____

-less
7 _____
8 _____

-ment
9 _____
10 _____

Name _____

# Spelling Spree

**Proofreading** Circle five misspelled Spelling Words in the letter. Then write each word correctly.

## Spelling Words

1. wonderful
2. countless
3. excitement
4. exactly
5. kindness
6. sleepless
7. mouthful
8. brightness
9. finally
10. government

Dear Mr. McBroom,

When I first tasted a mouthfull of your home-grown watermelon, I could hardly control my excitement! Its flavor was wunderful!! I knew I must have more. Now, after several sleepliss nights, I have finaly found you. I would like to buy the rest of your melons. Please do me the kindnes of answering as soon as possible.

Very truly yours,

*Gwendolyn Goldgrabber*

1 _____

2 _____

3 _____

4 _____

5 _____

**Analogies** Write the Spelling Word that completes each analogy.

6 Air is to weightless as stars are to _____.

7 Sergeant is to military as senator is to _____.

8 Perhaps is to definitely as approximately is to _____.

9 Yawning is to boredom as cheering is to _____.

10 Clouds are to darkness as sun is to _____.

**Heck's Revenge** Heck Jones plans to get even with McBroom by planting poison ivy seeds. On a separate sheet of paper, write a paragraph telling how McBroom might foil Heck's plan. Use Spelling Words from the list.

# Find the Farm

## Prepositions and Prepositional Phrases

When Josh McBroom sent a map to his friend, he forgot to include prepositions in his directions. Add the correct prepositions.

| about | by |
|-------|------|
| above | down |
| after | over |
| around | past |
| at | to |
| before | under |
| beside | |

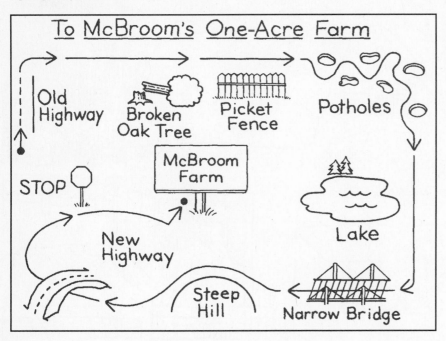

When you get _____ the old highway, make a right turn. Soon you will drive _____ a broken oak tree. Next, you will go _____ a picket fence. Drive very carefully _____ the potholes. As you drive _____ the lake, you will have a lovely view. Then, cross _____ a narrow bridge. Watch out as you drive _____ a steep hill. Next, pass _____ the new highway. Turn right immediately _____ the stop sign. Finally, you will be _____ the McBroom farm.

**More!** On a separate sheet of paper, write directions to tell how to get from the front of your school to your classroom. Include a prepositional phrase in each sentence. Then draw a map.

Name

# On and Around the Farm

## Prepositions and Prepositional Phrases

Write home about your visit to McBroom's farm. Write
five sentences describing life on the farm. Use a
prepositional phrase in each sentence.

| along | into |
|-------|------|
| around | near |
| beside | outside |
| by | over |
| down | past |
| during | up |
| in | without |

---
Name

# Let's Tell a Story!

## Story Ideas
Do any of these ideas make you think of a story?

A new friend          A rivalry between friends
On a spaceship        The score is tied
The missing page       The moose and the mosquito
A locked box          A mystery bus trip
Adventures of a pencil  A talking tree

## My Story Topics   Write five story ideas that you would like to write about.

_____

_____

_____

_____

_____

Ask yourself these questions about each idea.

Can I think of an interesting plot?

Will my audience enjoy reading about this?

Can I picture the setting and the characters clearly?

Will I enjoy writing about it?

Now circle the topic you will write about.

Name

# Who? Where? What?

Fill in the story map. Tell who your main characters are. Tell the setting, or where and when the story takes place. What problem do the characters deal with? What happens in the beginning, middle, and end? How do the characters solve the problem?

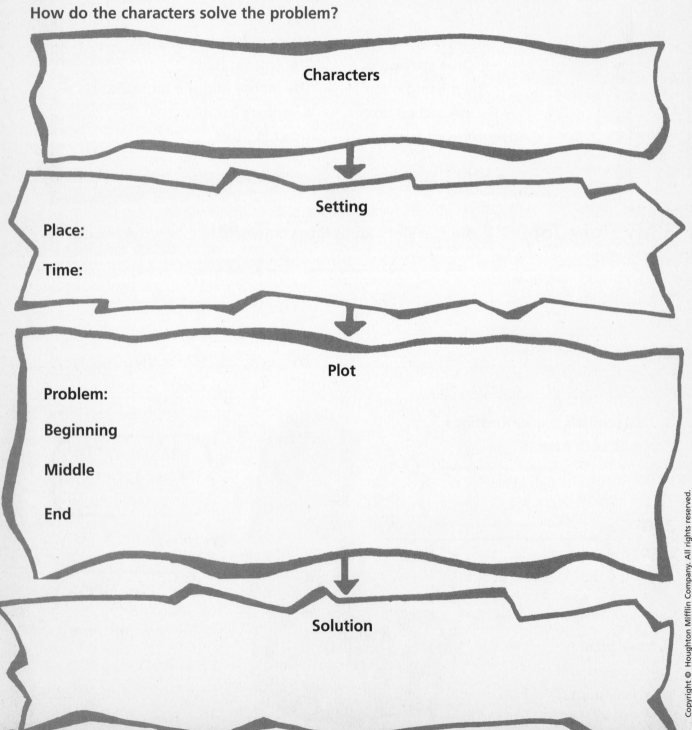

**Characters**

**Setting**

Place:

Time:

**Plot**

Problem:

Beginning

Middle

End

**Solution**

**Do You *Believe* This??**

Name

# Take Another Look

Reread your story to yourself and revise it, using the Revising Checklist. Then discuss your story with a classmate. Use the Questions for a Writing Conference to guide the discussion.

## Revising Checklist

**Ask yourself these questions about your story.**

❑ Did I introduce the main characters, setting, and problem in the beginning?

❑ Does each event relate to the problem?

❑ Did I use details and dialogue to show what the characters are like?

❑ Did I use details to make the setting and action interesting and clear?

❑ Does the ending resolve the problem in a way that makes sense?

## Questions for a Writing Conference

Use these questions to help you discuss your story.

• What do you like about this story?

• Are there parts that are unclear or do not seem to fit in? How could they be improved?

• Does the story *show* what the characters are like?

• Is the setting clear? Are more details needed?

• Where could dialogue be used to tell the action? to show what a character is like?

• Does the ending fit the characters and the story?

Write notes to help you remember ideas discussed in your writing conference.

**My Notes**

Name _____

# Dig Up the Past

**You are a scientist! The photos show your finds after a hard day of digging at the excavation. Use the words from the box to complete your log. Tell about your discoveries and what you did during the day.**

impression    skeletons
fossil        excavated
preserved     extinct

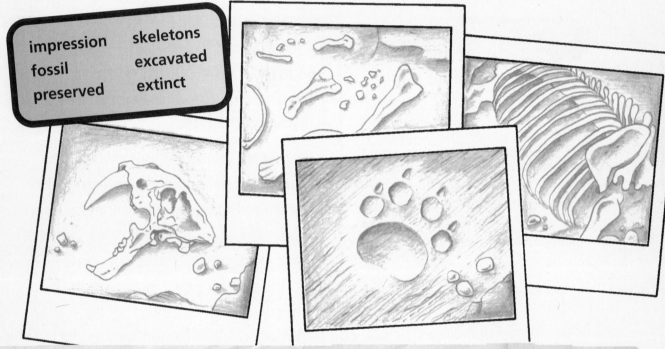

## Scientist's Log

Date: _____

Place: _____

Job: _____

What a day! After a hard morning spent chipping away at rock, I found _____

_____

_____

_____

_____

_____

_____

Name _____

# Sticky Pictures

Write a description of what is happening to the animal. Explain how the animal will become a fossil.

_____

_____

_____

_____

_____

_____

_____

_____

Write a description of what the men are doing. Explain what they do with the fossils.

_____

_____

_____

_____

_____

_____

_____

_____

_____

Do You *Believe* This?? **247**

Name

# Excavations Past and Present

What was the topic of *Trapped in Tar: Fossils from the Ice Age?*

What main idea is expressed in each photograph? Write the main ideas in the chart. Then list three details from the selection or the photos that support the main ideas.

| | |
|---|---|
| **Main idea:** | **Main idea:** |
| **Supporting details:** | **Supporting details:** |

On a separate piece of paper and using the information in the chart, write a brief summary of the selection.

Name

# Excavation Explanation

**Suppose you discovered some fossils in your neighborhood. Write an explanation telling how they would be excavated. Use the planner to help you organize your information. Then write your explanation.**

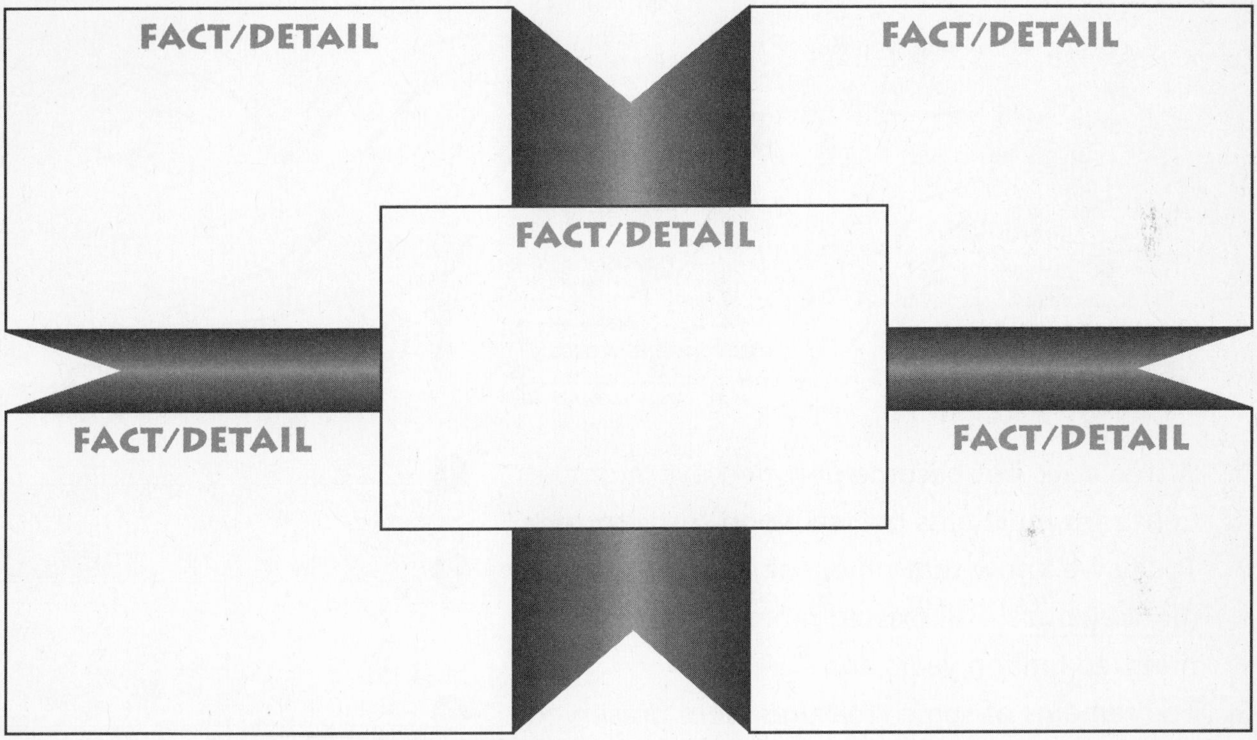
FACT/DETAIL
FACT/DETAIL
FACT/DETAIL
FACT/DETAIL
FACT/DETAIL

Name

# A Search for Meaning

Your friend doesn't know the meaning of some words in an article he's reading. Use context clues to help him figure them out and then write the meaning of each underlined word.

I'll help you find out.

What is my definition?

Ask me!

general context of sentence

unfamiliar word

appositive

1. "A tree does not become <u>petrified</u> overnight. Centuries must pass before wood turns to rock."

**1** _____

2. "Today we know that pine, oak, willow, and <u>monkey puzzle</u> all existed more than one hundred million years ago."

**2** _____

3. "The remains of some creatures were preserved in layers of mud that eventually hardened to form <u>sedimentary rock</u>."

**3** _____

4. "Prehistoric corals did not live together in large groups but were <u>solitary</u> animals."

**4** _____

5. "Dinosaurs may have developed from <u>archosaurs</u>, early reptiles."

**5** _____

6. "Perfectly preserved mammoths were excavated from frozen mud. Even their hair and skin were <u>intact</u>."

**6** _____

7. "Meat of the fossil mammoths looked good to eat, but its taste was actually <u>repugnant</u>."

**7** _____

8. "By studying fossils, paleontologists provide a clearer picture of extinct life forms, making the prehistoric past less <u>obscure</u>."

**8** _____

Name

# Ice Age Excavation

Five Ice Age mammals are buried in the tar pit. Write the vocabulary words in the grid in the order in which their definitions appear. Write one letter in each box and don't skip any boxes! Write the letters from the grid on the blanks, matching the number below each blank with the number in each grid box.

| decay | impression |
|-------|------------|
| excavated | preserved |
| immersed | ancient |
| fossil | embedded |
| skeletons | extinct |

a. extremely old

b. to break down; to rot

c. firmly placed in a surrounding substance

d. dug out of something

e. no longer existing

f. the hardened remains or imprint of a plant or animal from long ago

g. completely covered in liquid

h. a mark made by pressing

i. kept unharmed or undamaged

j. the frameworks of bones that support and protect the bodies of many animals

| 1 | 2 | 3 | 4 | 5 | 6 | 7 | 8 |
|---|---|---|---|---|---|---|---|
| 9 | 10 | 11 | 12 | 13 | 14 | 15 | 16 |
| 17 | 18 | 19 | 20 | 21 | 22 | 23 | 24 |
| 25 | 26 | 27 | 28 | 29 | 30 | 31 | 32 |
| 33 | 34 | 35 | 36 | 37 | 38 | 39 | 40 |
| 41 | 42 | 43 | 44 | 45 | 46 | 47 | 48 |
| 49 | 50 | 51 | 52 | 53 | 54 | 55 | 56 |
| 57 | 58 | 59 | 60 | 61 | 62 | 63 | 64 |
| 65 | 66 | 67 | 68 | 69 | 70 | 71 | 72 |
| 73 | 74 | 75 | 76 | 77 | 78 | | |

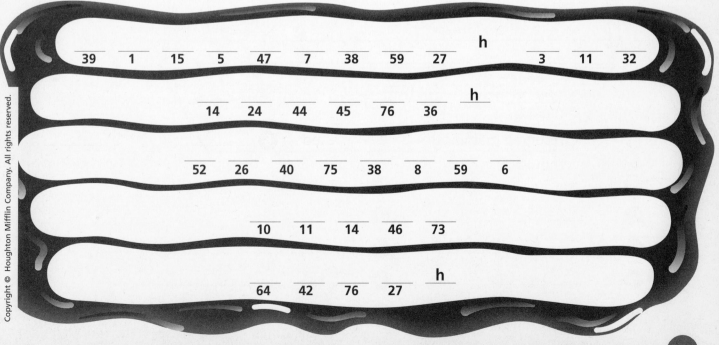

<u>   </u> <u>   </u> <u>   </u> <u>   </u> <u>   </u> <u>   </u> <u>   </u> <u>   </u> <u>   </u> <u> h </u> <u>   </u> <u>   </u> <u>   </u>

39   1   15   5   47   7   38   59   27      3   11   32

14   24   44   45   76   36   h

52   26   40   75   38   8   59   6

10   11   14   46   73

64   42   76   27   h

Do You *Believe* This?? **251**

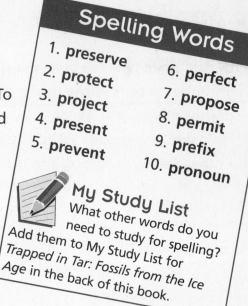

Name _____

# Prehistoric Puzzle

**The Prefixes *pre-*, *per-*, and *pro-*** Each Spelling Word has the prefix **pre-**, **per-**, or **pro-**. To spell a word with a prefix, think of the prefix and then the base word or the word root.

| Prefix | Meaning | Word |
|--------|---------|------|
| pre- | earlier; before | preserve |
| per- | through | perfect |
| pro- | forward; in front of | protect |

Make Spelling Words by drawing a line from each prefix on a bone fragment to the matching word part. Then write the words.

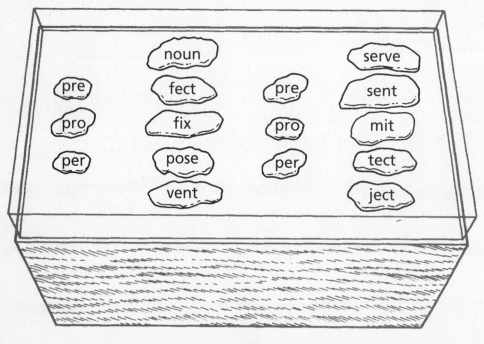

1  _____    6  _____

2  _____    7  _____

3  _____    8  _____

4  _____    9  _____

5  _____    10 _____

Name ........................................................

**Trapped in Tar:** Fossils from the Ice Age

SPELLING   The Prefixes *pre-*, *per-*, and *pro-*

# Spelling Spree

**Proofreading**  **Find and circle five misspelled Spelling Words in this test for new tour guides. Then write each word correctly.**

| Spelling Words |
| --- |
| 1. preserve     6. perfect |
| 2. protect      7. propose |
| 3. project      8. permit |
| 4. present      9. prefix |
| 5. prevent      10. pronoun |

- What does the museum feature at present?
- Why are animal skeletons often found in purfect condition?
- How does tar pretect and perserve animal remains?
- Why must scientists privent people from taking fossils from a dig site?
- How did scientists propos to save bone deposits that were uncovered when the new museum was being built?

1 _____
2 _____
3 _____
4 _____
5 _____

**Tar Puzzle**  **Find and circle the Spelling Word that is named in each clue. The word may appear across, down, or diagonally. Then write the words.**

6. *I, she,* or *it,* for example
7. a word part coming before a base word
8. at this time; now
9. allow
10. a large task or plan

```
P P M I T P R O J
P R O N O U N E E
R E O P O N K Y S
I F R J R U N D Y
P I P R E S E N T
O X P R O C T E C
A P E R M I T L T
```

6 _____      8 _____      10 _____

7 _____      9 _____

**Help Wanted**  A local museum must hire a paleontologist to direct fossil excavations and set up museum exhibits. On a separate sheet of paper, write a want ad. Include a description of the skills needed and the requirements of the job. Use Spelling Words from the list.

.......................................................................................................
Name

# This Place Is the Pits!

**Object Pronouns in Prepositional Phrases** You are in charge of training new tour guides for the La Brea tar pits. Your assistant has written a script but is unsure which object pronouns to use. Complete the script by filling in the correct object pronouns.

around us!

near him

beside her

under you

Hey! The tar is...

between them

Millions of years ago, pools of tar seeped to the surface of the earth. The tar was very sticky, and sometimes animals got stuck in _____. At first, the bones floated, but when the tar soaked through _____ , they sank to the bottom of the pit. They lay hidden for thousands of years. These tar pits once belonged to Captain G. Allen Hancock, so now this park is named after _____. It's time to begin our tour.

This is my partner, Felicia. Please walk behind her and _____. We are both wearing red badges, so it should be easy to keep track of _____. We both know the area well, so come to _____ or _____ with questions. We want to be helpful to _____. Remember, if you see any live sabertooth cats, please don't give food to _____. We, however, haven't had lunch, so you can give it to _____!

Name

# A Post Card from Rancho La Brea

**Using *I* and *me*** Julio wrote a friend after visiting
the La Brea tar pits. He used *I* or *me* ten times, but he
didn't always use them correctly. Use the delete sign ( ℒ )
to cross out his errors. Write the correct pronoun above
the line.

My brother and I
**Example:** ~~Me and my brother~~ will mail the post card.

Dear Juan,

Yesterday my family and me visited a place called the La Brea tar pits.
Me and Dad were the first ones to jump out of the car and take a look. It was fun.
Dad and I learned a lot about fossils. Of course, my little brother kept bothering Mom
and me. A tour guide stood beside another boy and I. The other boy and I had the
best view of things. When we got to the tar pits, we were careful. My brother and me
always stood behind Dad. Well, I hope your summer isn't too boring. Maybe next year
you and me can take a trip together. Look for Dad, Mom, and I next week.

See you soon,

*Julio*

**On a separate sheet of paper, rewrite the post card.**

Name

# Making a Do-You-Believe Comic Strip

In small groups, discuss stories you know that mix up the real with the make-believe. Think, for example, of science fiction stories and tall tales. Use one of those stories, or make up one of your own, and turn it into a comic strip. This page will help you plan your strip. First, list some possible ideas for the comic strip.

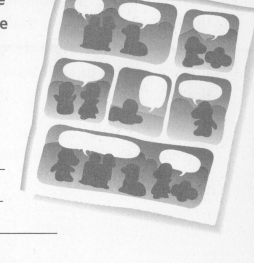

**1** _____

**2** _____

**3** _____

Pick the idea you like best. Make sure you have material for a Do-You-Believe strip.

• What is real in the story: _____

• What is unreal in the story: _____

Plan each frame, or box, in the comic strip. Try to make a story with interesting details.

• The first frame: _____

• The middle frames (as many as you need): _____

_____

• The final frame: _____

Discuss your story with your partners. When you are satisfied that you have a good Do-You-Believe story, draw your comic strip. Your strip can have just pictures or pictures with words.

## Checklist

☐ The comic strip has both real and make-believe ideas or events.

☐ It has details that make it an interesting story.

☐ It has a plot with a definite conclusion.

# STUDENT HANDBOOK

# STUDENT HANDBOOK

# Contents

**Independent Reading Log**                    **259**

**Spelling Guide**                             **263**

How to Study a Word                             263

Words Often Misspelled                          264

Take-Home Word Lists                            265

Spelling Guidelines                             279


**Grammar Guide: A Resource for Grammar,**     **284**
**Usage, Capitalization, and Punctuation**

Sentences                Abbreviations

Nouns                    Titles

Verbs                    Quotations

Adjectives               Capitalization

Adverbs                  Punctuation

Pronouns                 Problem Words

Prepositions and         Adjective and Adverb Usage
Prepositional
Phrases                  Pronoun Usage


**Proofreading Checklist**                     **316**


**Proofreading Marks**                         **316**

# INDEPENDENT READING LOG

Use this log to record the books or other materials you read on your own.

Date _____

Author _____

Title _____

Notes and Comments _____

_____

_____

_____

Date _____

Author _____

Title _____

Notes and Comments _____

_____

_____

_____

Date _____

Author _____

Title _____

Notes and Comments _____

_____

_____

_____

_____

Date _____

Author _____

Title _____

Notes and Comments _____

_____

_____

_____

_____

Date _____

Author _____

Title _____

Notes and Comments _____

_____

_____

_____

_____

Date _____

Author _____

Title _____

Notes and Comments _____

_____

_____

_____

Date _____

Author _____

Title _____

Notes and Comments _____

_____

_____

_____

Date _____

Author _____

Title _____

Notes and Comments _____

_____

_____

_____

Date _____

Author _____

Title _____

Notes and Comments _____

_____

_____

_____

_____

Date _____

Author _____

Title _____

Notes and Comments _____

_____

_____

_____

_____

Date _____

Author _____

Title _____

Notes and Comments _____

_____

_____

_____

_____

# How to Study a Word

**1 LOOK at the word.**

- What does the word mean?
- What letters are in the word?
- Name and touch each letter.

**2 SAY the word.**

- Listen for the consonant sounds.
- Listen for the vowel sounds.

**3 THINK about the word.**

- How is each sound spelled?
- Close your eyes and picture the word.
- What familiar spelling patterns do you see?
- Do you see any prefixes, suffixes, or other word parts?

**4 WRITE the word.**

- Think about the sounds and the letters.
- Form the letters correctly.

**5 CHECK the spelling.**

- Did you spell the word the same way it is spelled in your word list?
- If you did not spell the word correctly, write the word again.

# WORDS OFTEN MISSPELLED

| | | | | |
|---|---|---|---|---|
| accept | busy | fourth | nickel | to |
| ache | buy | Friday | ninety | too |
| again | by | friend | ninety-nine | tried |
| all right | calendar | goes | ninth | tries |
| almost | cannot | going | often | truly |
| already | can't | grammar | once | two |
| although | careful | guard | other | tying |
| always | catch | guess | people | unknown |
| angel | caught | guide | principal | until |
| angle | chief | half | quiet | unusual |
| | | | | |
| answer | children | haven't | quit | wasn't |
| argue | choose | hear | quite | wear |
| asked | chose | heard | really | weather |
| aunt | color | heavy | receive | Wednesday |
| author | cough | height | rhythm | weird |
| awful | cousin | here | right | we'll |
| babies | decide | hers | Saturday | we're |
| been | divide | hole | stretch | weren't |
| believe | does | hoping | surely | we've |
| bother | don't | hour | their | where |
| | | | | |
| bought | early | its | theirs | which |
| break | enough | it's | there | whole |
| breakfast | every | January | they're | witch |
| breathe | exact | let's | they've | won't |
| broken | except | listen | those | wouldn't |
| brother | excite | loose | though | write |
| brought | expect | lose | thought | writing |
| bruise | February | minute | through | written |
| build | finally | muscle | tied | you're |
| business | forty | neighbor | tired | yours |

## Voyager: An Adventure to the Edge of the Solar System

### Spelling long u

| yōō| or → | huge |
| lōō| | blue |
| | smooth |
| | juice |
| | group |

### Spelling Words

1. huge
2. blue
3. smooth
4. clue
5. ooze
6. group
7. juice
8. route
9. rude
10. bruise

### Challenge Words

1. continue
2. through
3. include
4. pursue
5. attitude

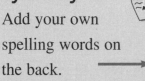

### My Study List

Add your own spelling words on the back. →

---

## Arctic Explorer: The Story of Matthew Henson

### Spelling Long i and Long o

| |ī| → | drive, sight |
| |ō| → | froze, goal, snow |

### Spelling Words

1. snow
2. goal
3. froze
4. sight
5. drive
6. wrote
7. load
8. midnight
9. prize
10. narrow

### Challenge Words

1. highway
2. dynamite
3. realize
4. twilight
5. cocoa

### My Study List

Add your own spelling words on the back. →

---

## James and the Giant Peach

### Spelling Long a and Long e

| |ā| → | wake, bait, sway |
| |ē| → | peach, between |

### Spelling Words

1. peach
2. bait
3. beast
4. between
5. afraid
6. wake
7. sway
8. scale
9. speed
10. stray

### Challenge Words

1. seagull
2. explain
3. appeal
4. dismay
5. succeed

### My Study List

Add your own spelling words on the back. →

## My Study List

1. _____
2. _____
3. _____
4. _____
5. _____
6. _____
7. _____
8. _____
9. _____
10. _____

## Selection Vocabulary

You may want to use these words in your own writing.

1. frantic
2. exhorting
3. lunge
4. pandemonium
5. tethered
6. aghast

## How to Study a Word

LOOK at the word.
SAY the word.
THINK about the word.
WRITE the word.
CHECK the spelling.

---

## My Study List

1. _____
2. _____
3. _____
4. _____
5. _____
6. _____
7. _____
8. _____
9. _____
10. _____

## Selection Vocabulary

You may want to use these words in your own writing.

1. expedition
2. sledges
3. lead
4. ice floe
5. interpreter

## How to Study a Word

LOOK at the word.
SAY the word.
THINK about the word.
WRITE the word.
CHECK the spelling.

---

## My Study List

1. _____
2. _____
3. _____
4. _____
5. _____
6. _____
7. _____
8. _____
9. _____
10. _____

## Selection Vocabulary

You may want to use these words in your own writing.

1. atmosphere
2. gravity
3. orbit
4. particles
5. meteorites
6. comet

## How to Study a Word

LOOK at the word.
SAY the word.
THINK about the word.
WRITE the word.
CHECK the spelling.

## Adiós falcón/Good-bye, Falcon

### The Vowel + r Sounds in bird

lûrl ➤ perch, bird, return, learn, world

### Spelling Words

1. bird
2. perch
3. return
4. learn
5. hurt
6. world
7. prefer
8. firm
9. worth
10. early

### Challenge Words

1. perfume
2. murmur
3. emergency
4. interpret
5. universe

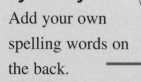

**My Study List**

Add your own spelling words on the back. ➤

---

## The Midnight Fox

### More Vowel + r Sounds

lôrl ➤ porch, before, roar

lîrl ➤ peer, fear

### Spelling Words

1. fear
2. before
3. porch
4. force
5. clear
6. corner
7. roar
8. peer
9. soar
10. steer

### Challenge Words

1. orchard
2. forward
3. ordeal
4. disappear
5. volunteer

**My Study List**

Add your own spelling words on the back. ➤

---

## Wolves

### Vowel + r Sounds

lârl ➤ bare, hair

lärl ➤ sharp

### Spelling Words

1. sharp
2. bark
3. hair
4. bare
5. startle
6. pair
7. care
8. share
9. apart
10. stare

### Challenge Words

1. marvelous
2. arctic
3. scarce
4. argument
5. hierarchy

**My Study List**

Add your own spelling words on the back. ➤

Name _____

 **My Study List**

1. _____
2. _____
3. _____
4. _____
5. _____
6. _____
7. _____
8. _____
9. _____
10. _____

## Selection Vocabulary

You may want to use these words in your own writing.

1. adaptable
2. dominance
3. hierarchy
4. domesticated
5. submissive

## How to Study a Word

LOOK at the word.
SAY the word.
THINK about the word.
WRITE the word.
CHECK the spelling.

Name _____

 **My Study List**

1. _____
2. _____
3. _____
4. _____
5. _____
6. _____
7. _____
8. _____
9. _____
10. _____

## Selection Vocabulary

You may want to use these words in your own writing.

1. dread
2. discouraged
3. hopelessness
4. desperate
5. anxiously
6. doomed

## How to Study a Word

LOOK at the word.
SAY the word.
THINK about the word.
WRITE the word.
CHECK the spelling.

Name _____

 **My Study List**

1. _____
2. _____
3. _____
4. _____
5. _____
6. _____
7. _____
8. _____
9. _____
10. _____

## Selection Vocabulary

You may want to use these words in your own writing.

1. endure
2. captivity
3. warily
4. clashed
5. liberty

## How to Study a Word

LOOK at the word.
SAY the word.
THINK about the word.
WRITE the word.
CHECK the spelling.

## Me, Mop, and the Moondance Kid

### Final Schwa + l Sounds

|əl| or
|l| ➔ eagle, level, special

### Spelling Words

1. eagle
2. example
3. special
4. double
5. single
6. signal
7. level
8. normal
9. towel
10. model

### Challenge Words

1. national
2. actual
3. duffel
4. cancel
5. natural

### My Study List

Add your own spelling words on the back.

## Like Jake and Me

### Final Schwa + r Sounds

|ər| ➔ spider
color
collar

### Spelling Words

1. spider
2. silver
3. color
4. feather
5. bother
6. collar
7. cover
8. quarter
9. flavor
10. sugar

### Challenge Words

1. shudder
2. swagger
3. poplar
4. nectar
5. regular

### My Study List

Add your own spelling words on the back.

## In the Year of the Boar and Jackie Robinson

### The Vowel Sounds in shout and wall

|ou| ➔ shout, allow
|ô| ➔ dawn, fault, wall

### Spelling Words

1. shout
2. wall
3. allow
4. counter
5. although
6. fault
7. frown
8. pause
9. dawn
10. straw

### Challenge Words

1. announce
2. throughout
3. eyebrows
4. awkward
5. autumn

### My Study List

Add your own spelling words on the back.

### My Study List

1. _____
2. _____
3. _____
4. _____
5. _____
6. _____
7. _____
8. _____
9. _____
10. _____

### Selection Vocabulary

You may want to use these words in your own writing.

1. ambassador
2. foreign
3. foreigner
4. reputation
5. escapade

### How to Study a Word

LOOK at the word.
SAY the word.
THINK about the word.
WRITE the word.
CHECK the spelling.

### My Study List

1. _____
2. _____
3. _____
4. _____
5. _____
6. _____
7. _____
8. _____
9. _____
10. _____

### Selection Vocabulary

You may want to use these words in your own writing.

1. gasped
2. grappled
3. swaggered
4. crouched
5. thundered

### How to Study a Word

LOOK at the word.
SAY the word.
THINK about the word.
WRITE the word.
CHECK the spelling.

### My Study List

1. _____
2. _____
3. _____
4. _____
5. _____
6. _____
7. _____
8. _____
9. _____
10. _____

### Selection Vocabulary

You may want to use these words in your own writing.

1. backstop
2. foul
3. play-offs
4. series
5. squad

### How to Study a Word

LOOK at the word.
SAY the word.
THINK about the word.
WRITE the word.
CHECK the spelling.

## Earthquakes

### The VCCV and VCV Patterns

VC|CV ➔ suf|fer, sur|face

V|CV ➔ to|tal

VC|V ➔ dam|age

### Spelling Words

1. damage
2. surface
3. entire
4. solid
5. total
6. object
7. notice
8. suffer
9. modern
10. mirror

### Challenge Words

1. tremor
2. collapse
3. occur
4. intense
5. focus

### My Study List

Add your own spelling words on the back. ➔

---

## Night of the Twisters

### Compound Words

**Compound words** can be written as one word, as a hyphenated word, or as separate words.

### Spelling Words

1. hallway
2. upstairs
3. flashlight
4. everything
5. driveway
6. built-in
7. first aid
8. baby-sit
9. already
10. all right

### Challenge Words

1. heartbeat
2. weather station
3. freight train
4. civil defense
5. handkerchief

### My Study List

Add your own spelling words on the back. ➔

---

## Felita

### Homophones

**Homophones** are words that sound alike but have different spellings and meanings.

### Spelling Words

1. seen
2. scene
3. wear
4. where
5. bow
6. bough
7. great
8. grate
9. fair
10. fare

### Challenge Words

1. raise
2. rays
3. raze
4. principal
5. principle

### My Study List

Add your own spelling words on the back. ➔

Name _____

 **My Study List**

1. _____
2. _____
3. _____
4. _____
5. _____
6. _____
7. _____
8. _____
9. _____
10. _____

## Selection Vocabulary

You may want to use these words in your own writing.

1. audition
2. heroine
3. recited
4. script
5. imitated
6. casting

## How to Study a Word

LOOK at the word.
SAY the word.
THINK about the word.
WRITE the word.
CHECK the spelling.

272

Name _____

 **My Study List**

1. _____
2. _____
3. _____
4. _____
5. _____
6. _____
7. _____
8. _____
9. _____
10. _____

## Selection Vocabulary

You may want to use these words in your own writing.

1. sobering
2. jolt
3. jammed
4. huddled
5. head-on
6. flickering

## How to Study a Word

LOOK at the word.
SAY the word.
THINK about the word.
WRITE the word.
CHECK the spelling.

272

Name _____

 **My Study List**

1. _____
2. _____
3. _____
4. _____
5. _____
6. _____
7. _____
8. _____
9. _____
10. _____

## Selection Vocabulary

You may want to use these words in your own writing.

1. colliding
2. friction
3. heaves
4. strains
5. stresses

## How to Study a Word

LOOK at the word.
SAY the word.
THINK about the word.
WRITE the word.
CHECK the spelling.

272

## Children of the Wild West

### Changing Final *y* to *i*

If a base word ends with a consonant and **y**, change the **y** to **i** when adding an ending or a suffix.

### Spelling Words

1. countries
2. supplied
3. happiness
4. hurried
5. angrier
6. enemies
7. tiniest
8. nastiest
9. grassier
10. friendliness

### Challenge Words

1. treaties
2. territories
3. satisfied
4. dignified
5. atrocities

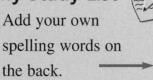

### My Study List

Add your own spelling words on the back. →

---

## Along the Santa Fe Trail

### Adding *-ed* or *-ing*

decide + **ed** = decid**ed**
stare + **ing** = star**ing**
depart + **ed** = depart**ed**
plan + **ing** = plan**ning**

### Spelling Words

1. planning
2. decided
3. departed
4. staring
5. offered
6. slipping
7. numbered
8. scattered
9. healing
10. knitted

### Challenge Words

1. altered
2. clutching
3. drenching
4. lumbered
5. resembled

### My Study List

Add your own spelling words on the back. →

---

## The Story of the Challenger *Disaster*

### The VCCCV Pattern

VC|CCV → far|ther
VC|CCV → ex|plode
VCC|CV → sand|wich

### Spelling Words

1. explode
2. instant
3. control
4. explore
5. address
6. struggle
7. express
8. empty
9. farther
10. sandwich

### Challenge Words

1. shuttle
2. approach
3. throttle
4. exclaim
5. congress

### My Study List

Add your own spelling words on the back. →

Name _____

 **My Study List**

1. _____
2. _____
3. _____
4. _____
5. _____
6. _____
7. _____
8. _____
9. _____
10. _____

## Selection Vocabulary

You may want to use these words in your own writing.

1. mourned
2. memorial
3. tribute
4. commemorate
5. grief
6. sympathy
7. tragedy

## How to Study a Word

LOOK at the word.
SAY the word.
THINK about the word.
WRITE the word.
CHECK the spelling.

Name _____

 **My Study List**

1. _____
2. _____
3. _____
4. _____
5. _____
6. _____
7. _____
8. _____
9. _____
10. _____

## Selection Vocabulary

You may want to use these words in your own writing.

1. epidemic
2. emigrant
3. vast
4. wallows
5. caravan
6. mesa
7. desolate

## How to Study a Word

LOOK at the word.
SAY the word.
THINK about the word.
WRITE the word.
CHECK the spelling.

Name _____

 **My Study List**

1. _____
2. _____
3. _____
4. _____
5. _____
6. _____
7. _____
8. _____
9. _____
10. _____

## Selection Vocabulary

You may want to use these words in your own writing.

1. customs
2. sacred
3. myths
4. primitive
5. civilization
6. traditional
7. culture

## How to Study a Word

LOOK at the word.
SAY the word.
THINK about the word.
WRITE the word.
CHECK the spelling.

## Willie Bea and the Time the Martians Landed

### The Prefixes *un-, re-,* and *dis-*

un- → **un**clear
re- → **re**move
dis- → **dis**tant

### Spelling Words

1. unclear
2. distant
3. untrue
4. discomfort
5. remove
6. untangle
7. unsure
8. remind
9. disagree
10. report

### Challenge Words

1. unfortunate
2. disbelief
3. unnecessary
4. uneasily
5. disenchantment

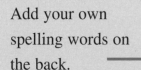

**My Study List**

Add your own spelling words on the back. →

---

## La Bamba

### The Prefixes *in-* and *con-*

in- → **in**hale
im- → **im**mediate
con- → **con**fuse
com- → **com**pete

### Spelling Words

1. impress
2. confuse
3. conduct
4. inhale
5. intent
6. command
7. immediate
8. compete
9. impolite
10. connect

### Challenge Words

1. confident
2. commotion
3. instrument
4. conversation
5. immigrant

**My Study List**

Add your own spelling words on the back. →

---

## Pecos Bill

### Adding *-ion*

act → act**ion**
create → creat**ion**

### Spelling Words

1. act
2. action
3. create
4. creation
5. direct
6. direction
7. possess
8. possession
9. narrate
10. narration

### Challenge Words

1. progress
2. progression
3. adopt
4. adoption

**My Study List**

Add your own spelling words on the back. →

Name _____

## My Study List

1. _____
2. _____
3. _____
4. _____
5. _____
6. _____
7. _____
8. _____
9. _____
10. _____

## Selection Vocabulary

You may want to use these words in your own writing.

1. homestead
2. stagecoaches
3. cowpoke
4. hootenanny
5. coyotes

## How to Study a Word

LOOK at the word.
SAY the word.
THINK about the word.
WRITE the word.
CHECK the spelling.

276

---

Name _____

## My Study List

1. _____
2. _____
3. _____
4. _____
5. _____
6. _____
7. _____
8. _____
9. _____
10. _____

## Selection Vocabulary

You may want to use these words in your own writing.

1. pantomime
2. limelight
3. talent
4. debut
5. duo
6. forty-five record

## How to Study a Word

LOOK at the word.
SAY the word.
THINK about the word.
WRITE the word.
CHECK the spelling.

276

---

Name _____

## My Study List

1. _____
2. _____
3. _____
4. _____
5. _____
6. _____
7. _____
8. _____
9. _____
10. _____

## Selection Vocabulary

You may want to use these words in your own writing.

1. Martians
2. alien
3. Venus
4. outlandish
5. universe

## How to Study a Word

LOOK at the word.
SAY the word.
THINK about the word.
WRITE the word.
CHECK the spelling.

276

*Trapped in Tar: Fossils from the Ice Age*

## The Prefixes *pre-, per-,* and *pro-*

pre- ➤ **pre**serve
per- ➤ **per**fect
pro- ➤ **pro**tect

## Spelling Words

1. preserve
2. protect
3. project
4. present
5. prevent
6. perfect
7. propose
8. permit
9. prefix
10. pronoun

## Challenge Words

1. precise
2. procedure
3. persuade
4. prohibit
5. perspective

## My Study List

Add your own spelling words on the back. ➤

Take-Home Word Lists

*McBroom Tells the Truth*

## Words with Suffixes

-ly ➤ exact**ly**
-ful ➤ wonder**ful**
-ness ➤ kind**ness**
-less ➤ count**less**
-ment ➤ excite**ment**

## Spelling Words

1. wonderful
2. countless
3. excitement
4. exactly
5. kindness
6. sleepless
7. mouthful
8. brightness
9. finally
10. government

## Challenge Words

1. positively
2. disappoint
3. gentleness
4. occasionally
5. anxiously

## My Study List

Add your own spelling words on the back. ➤

Name _____

 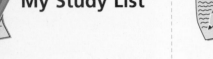  **My Study List**

1. _____
2. _____
3. _____
4. _____
5. _____
6. _____
7. _____
8. _____
9. _____
10. _____

## Selection Vocabulary

You may want to use these words in your own writing.

1. deed
2. foreclose
3. legal
4. loophole
5. bargain
6. profit

## How to Study a Word

LOOK at the word.
SAY the word.
THINK about the word.
WRITE the word.
CHECK the spelling.

---

Name _____

**My Study List**

1. _____
2. _____
3. _____
4. _____
5. _____
6. _____
7. _____
8. _____
9. _____
10. _____

## Selection Vocabulary

You may want to use these words in your own writing.

1. fossil
2. excavate
3. extinct
4. impression
5. preserved
6. skeletons

## How to Study a Word

LOOK at the word.
SAY the word.
THINK about the word.
WRITE the word.
CHECK the spelling.

## SPELLING GUIDELINES

### Short Vowel Patterns

| | | |
|---|---|---|
| **1.** A short vowel sound is usually spelled *a, e, i, o,* or *u* and is followed by a consonant sound. | **a**sk<br>n**e**xt<br>m**i**x | l**o**ck<br>sh**u**t |
| **2.** The short *e* sound can be spelled with the pattern *ea.* | m**ea**nt | |
| **3.** The short *u* sound can be spelled with the pattern *ou* or *o.* | t**ou**ch | n**o**thing |

### Long Vowel Sounds

| | | |
|---|---|---|
| **4.** The long *a* sound can be spelled with the pattern *a*-consonant-*e, ai, ay,* or *ea.* | w**a**k**e**<br>b**ai**t | sw**ay**<br>gr**ea**t |
| **5.** The long *e* sound is often spelled with the pattern *e*-consonant-*e, ea,* or *ee.* | th**e**s**e**<br>p**ea**ch | sp**ee**d |
| **6.** The long *e* sound at the end of a word may be spelled *y.* | penn**y** | funn**y** |
| **7.** The long *i* sound can be spelled with the pattern *i*-consonant-*e, igh,* or *ie.* | dr**i**v**e**<br>s**igh**t | t**ie** |
| **8.** The long *i* sound at the end of a word may be spelled *y.* | cr**y** | repl**y** |
| **9.** The long *o* sound can be spelled with the pattern *o*-consonant-*e, oa,* or *ow.* | fr**o**z**e**<br>g**oa**l | sn**ow** |
| **10.** The long *u* sound |y͞o͞o| or |o͞o| may be spelled with the pattern *u*-consonant-*e, ew, ue, oo, ou,* or *ui.* | h**u**g**e**<br>gr**ew**<br>bl**ue** | **oo**ze<br>gr**ou**p<br>j**ui**ce |

### Other Vowel Sounds

| | | |
|---|---|---|
| **11.** The sound |ou| is often spelled with the pattern *ow* or *ou.* | fr**ow**n | c**ou**nter |
| **12.** The sound |oi| is spelled with the pattern *oi* or *oy.* | n**oi**se | enj**oy** |

## Other Vowel Sounds (continued)

13. The vowel sound in *walk* can be spelled with the pattern *a* before *l, aw, au, ough,* or *augh.*

    **al**though    th**ough**t
    d**aw**n      c**augh**t
    p**au**se

14. The vowel sound in *cook* may be spelled with the pattern *oo* or *u.*

    w**oo**ds    p**u**ll

## Vowel + *r* Sounds

15. The vowel + **r** sounds you hear in *sharp* can be spelled with the pattern *ar.*

    st**ar**tle

16. The vowel + **r** sounds you hear in *hair* can be spelled with the pattern *are* or *air.*

    sh**are**    p**air**

17. The vowel + **r** sounds you hear in *peer* can be spelled with the pattern *ear* or *eer.*

    f**ear**    st**eer**

18. The vowel + **r** sounds you hear in *roar* can be spelled with the patterns *or, ore,* and *oar.*

    p**or**ch    s**oar**
    bef**ore**

19. The vowel + *r* sounds you hear in *perch* can be spelled with the pattern *er, ir, ur, ear,* or *or.*

    pref**er**    l**ear**n
    b**ir**d      w**or**ld
    ret**ur**n

## Consonant Sounds

20. The |s| sound you hear in *city* may be spelled *c* when the *c* is followed by *i* or *e.* The |s| sound at the end of a word is often spelled with the pattern *ce.*

    **ci**ty    on**ce**
    **ci**rcle    sli**ce**

21. The |j| sound you hear in *just* can be spelled with the consonant *j,* the pattern *dge,* or with the consonant *g* followed by *e.*

    **j**ust    lar**ge**
    **j**am     a**ge**
    ed**ge**

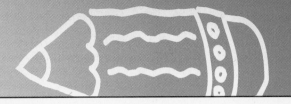
## Syllable Patterns

22. The schwa + *r* sounds that you hear in *spider* are often spelled with the pattern *er, or,* or *ar.*

    feath**er**  coll**ar**
    flav**or**

23. The schwa + *l* sounds that you hear in *double* can be spelled with the pattern *al, il, le,* or *el.*

    sign**al**  eag**le**
    gerb**il**  tow**el**

24. Some two-syllable words have the vowel-consonant-vowel pattern (VCV), and begin with the short vowel pattern. Divide a word with this pattern after the consonant to find the syllables. Look for spelling patterns you have learned. Spell the word by syllables.

    dam|age
    sol|id

25. Some two-syllable words have the vowel-consonant-vowel pattern (VCV), and the first syllable ends with a vowel sound. Divide a word with this pattern before the consonant to find the syllables. Look for spelling patterns you have learned. Spell the word by syllables.

    to|tal
    no|tice

26. Some two-syllable words have the vowel-consonant-consonant-vowel pattern (VCCV). Divide a word with this pattern between the two consonants to find the syllables. Look for spelling patterns you have learned. Spell the word by syllables.

    sur|face
    mir|ror

27. Some two-syllable words have the vowel-consonant-consonant-consonant-vowel (VCCCV) pattern. In these words, when two different consonants spell one sound, as in *farther*, or form a cluster, as in *control*, divide these words into syllables before or after those two consonants. Look for spelling patterns you have learned. Spell the word by syllables.

    VC|CCV    VCC|CV
    in|stant  sand|wich
    ex|plore  emp|ty

## Word Endings

**28.** If a base word ends with *e*, drop the *e* before adding the ending *-ed* or *-ing*.

decid**e**-decid**ed**
star**e**-star**ing**

**29.** If a base word ends with a vowel and a single consonant, double the consonant before adding *-ed* or *-ing*.

kni**t**-kni**tted**
sli**p**-sli**pping**

**30.** If a base word ends with a double consonant, don't change the spelling of the base word when adding *-ed* or *-ing*.

fo**ld**-fold**ed**
ru**sh**-rush**ed**

**31.** When *-ed* or *-ing* is added to a two-syllable word, the consonant is usually not doubled.

depart-depart**ed**
scatter-scatter**ed**

**32.** When a base word ends with a consonant and *y*, change the *y* to *i* before adding *-es, -ed, -er, -est,* or *-ness.*

countr**y**-countr**ies**
suppl**y**-suppl**ied**
angr**y**-angr**ier**
tin**y**-tin**iest**
happ**y**-happ**iness**

**33.** Add *s* to most words to name more than one. Add *es* to words that end with *s, x, sh,* or *ch* to name more than one thing.

trips       wi<u>sh</u>**es**
bu<u>s</u>**es**      pea<u>ch</u>**es**
bo<u>x</u>**es**

## Prefixes and Suffixes

**34.** A **prefix** is a word part added to the beginning of a base word or word root.

**re**read      **con**fuse
**un**fair      **com**pete
**dis**like      **pre**serve
**in**hale      **per**fect
**im**mediate **pro**tect

**35.** A **suffix** is a word part added to the end of a base word or word root.

thought**ful** home**less**
soft**ly**      good**ness**
writ**er**      excite**ment**

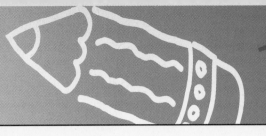

### Special Spellings

**36. Homophones** are words that sound alike but have different meanings and spellings.

bough-bow
seen-scene

**37.** In **contractions**, an apostrophe takes the place of the letters that are dropped.

have not-haven't
should not-shouldn't

**38.** A **compound word** is made up of two or more smaller words. It can be written as one word, as two words joined by a hyphen, or as two separate words.

sunlight    pen pal
great-aunt

**39. Silent consonants** are consonants that are not pronounced.

| | |
|---|---|
| wrong | island |
| palm | often |
| honest | knew |
| knee | half |
| climb | answer |

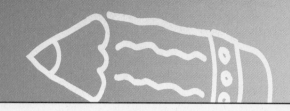

# GRAMMAR GUIDE

## SENTENCES

### Definition

A **sentence** is a group of words that expresses a complete thought. It has a subject (who or what) and a predicate (what the subject does or is). A sentence begins with a capital letter.

> **L**ightning flashed in the sky.      **T**he alert ranger spotted the fire.

- A group of words that does not express a complete thought is called a **sentence fragment.** A fragment is not a sentence. A fragment is missing a subject, a predicate, or both.

> Flashed in the sky.      The alert ranger.
> During the storm.      When the tree fell.

### Kinds of Sentences

There are four kinds of sentences.

- A **declarative sentence** tells something. It ends with a period.

> **D**eserts are dry**.**

- An **interrogative sentence** asks something. It ends with a question mark.

> **D**o you like deserts**?**

- An **imperative sentence** gives an order. It ends with a period.

> **A**lways carry water**.**

- An **exclamatory sentence** expresses strong feeling. It ends with an exclamation point.

> **H**ow hot it was**!**      **I**t was so hot**!**

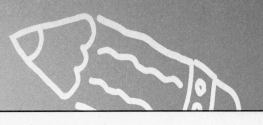

## Subjects and Predicates

Every sentence has a **subject** and a **predicate.**

- The **subject** tells whom or what the sentence is about. The **complete subject** includes all the words in the subject. It may be either one word or more than one word.

  **The pilots of the plane** waved.     **They** were preparing for take-off.

- The **simple subject** is the main word or words in the complete subject.

  The <u>pilots</u> of the plane waved.     <u>South America</u> is their destination.

- In an imperative sentence the subject *you* is understood.

  (You) Please bring your camera.

- The **predicate** tells what the subject is or does. The **complete predicate** includes all the words in the predicate. It may be either one word or more than one word.

  Captain Ortega **is a good pilot.**     The large jet **landed.**

- The **simple predicate** is the main word or words in the complete predicate.

  Two helicopters <u>landed</u> there.     They <u>have landed</u> there before.

## Run-on Sentences

A **run-on sentence** is two or more sentences that are run together incorrectly.

- Correct a run-on sentence by writing each complete thought as a separate sentence.

  RUN-ON:   Electricians often wear rubber gloves electricity cannot
            go through rubber.

  CORRECTED:   Electricians often wear rubber gloves. Electricity cannot
               go through rubber.

- Correct a run-on sentence by making it into a compound sentence (using *and, but,* or *or*). In a compound sentence, the two parts should be related.

  RUN-ON:   Some jobs require special clothing these clothes provide protection.

  CORRECTED:   Some jobs require special clothing, **and** these clothes provide
               protection.

### Run-on Sentences (continued)

- Correct a run-on that has three parts by dividing it into one compound sentence and one short sentence.

> RUN-ON: Some firefighters wear flameproof suits the suits are coated with metal they totally cover the firefighter.

> CORRECTED: Some firefighters wear flameproof suits. (*short*) The suits are coated with metal, **and** they totally cover the firefighter. (*compound*)

## NOUNS

### Definition

A **noun** names a person, a place, a thing, or an idea.

| Nouns | | |
|---|---|---|
| **Persons** | boy<br>student | writer<br>Li Chen |
| **Places** | lake<br>Fenway Park | Olympia<br>mountain |
| **Things** | boat<br>calendar | sweater<br>*Little Women* |
| **Ideas** | truth<br>freedom | belief<br>happiness |

## Common and Proper Nouns

A **common noun** names any person, place, or thing. A **proper noun** names a particular person, place, or thing. Capitalize proper nouns. Capitalize each important word in proper nouns of more than one word.

### Common and Proper Nouns

| Common nouns | Proper nouns | Common nouns | Proper nouns |
| --- | --- | --- | --- |
| street | North Drive | river | Hudson River |
| city | Vancouver | building | White House |
| state | Maryland | law | Bill of Rights |
| continent | Asia | author | Walter Dean Myers |
| ocean | Arctic Ocean | holiday | Fourth of July |
| mountain | Mt. McKinley | month | November |
| lake | Great Salt Lake | day | Monday |

## Singular and Plural Nouns

**Singular nouns** name one person, place, or thing,

> The **farmer** drove to the **market** with the **box**.

**Plural nouns** name more than one person, place, or thing.

> The **farmers** drove to the **markets** with the **boxes**.

- Form the plural of most nouns by adding *s* or *es*. Look at the ending of a singular noun to decide how to form the plural. Some nouns have special plural forms.

(See chart on the next page.)

## Singular and Plural Nouns (continued)

### Rules for Forming Plural Nouns

| | | |
|---|---|---|
| **1. Most singular nouns:** Add *s*. | street | street**s** |
| | house | house**s** |
| **2. Nouns ending with *s*, *x*, *ch*, or *sh*:** Add *es*. | dress | dress**es** |
| | ax | ax**es** |
| | bench | bench**es** |
| | dish | dish**es** |
| **3. Nouns ending with a vowel and *y*:** Add *s*. | valley | valley**s** |
| | joy | joy**s** |
| **4. Nouns ending with a consonant and *y*:** Change the *y* to *i* and add *es*. | city | cit**ies** |
| | cranberry | cranberr**ies** |
| **5. Nouns ending in *f* or *fe*:** Change the *f* to *v* and add *es* to some nouns. Add *s* to other nouns. | life | li**ves** |
| | calf | cal**ves** |
| | leaf | lea**ves** |
| | cliff | cliff**s** |
| **6. Nouns ending with a vowel and *o*:** Add *s*. | rodeo | rodeo**s** |
| | studio | studio**s** |
| | radio | radio**s** |
| **7. Nouns ending with a consonant and *o*:** Add *s* to some nouns. Add *es* to other nouns. | solo | solo**s** |
| | piano | piano**s** |
| | hero | hero**es** |
| | echo | echo**es** |
| | tomato | tomato**es** |
| **8. Nouns that have special plural spellings** | woman | wom**en** |
| | mouse | m**ice** |
| | foot | f**eet** |
| | ox | ox**en** |
| **9. Nouns that remain the same in the singular and the plural** | sheep | sheep |
| | moose | moose |
| | trout | trout |
| | deer | deer |

## GRAMMAR GUIDE

### Singular and Plural Possessive Nouns

A **singular possessive noun** shows that one person, place, or thing has or owns something.

- To form the possessive of a singular noun, add an apostrophe and *s*.

  the car**'s** tires          a student**'s** papers          Rosa**'s** opinion

A **plural possessive noun** shows that more than one person, place, or thing has or owns something.

- If a plural noun ends with *s*, add only an apostrophe.

  the cars**'** horns          two students**'** books          two girls**'** ideas

- If a plural noun does not end with *s*, add an apostrophe and *s*.

  the children**'s** choice          the oxen**'s** tracks          the people**'s** cheers

| Singular | Singular Possessive | Plural | Plural Possessive |
|----------|---------------------|--------|-------------------|
| girl | girl's | girls | girls' |
| calf | calf's | calves | calves' |
| pony | pony's | ponies | ponies' |
| child | child's | children | children's |
| mouse | mouse's | mice | mice's |
| deer | deer's | deer | deer's |

### VERBS

### Definition

A **verb** shows action or a state of being. It is the main word in the predicate.

ACTION: The fire **burns** brightly.          BEING: It **is** warm.

### Action Verbs and Direct Objects

An **action verb** shows what the subject does or did. Action verbs can also show action that you cannot see.

> Roberta **swings** at the ball.     Roberta **ran** to first base.
> The coach **thought** about the players in the field.

A **direct object** is a noun or a pronoun in the predicate that receives the action of the verb.

- Direct objects follow action verbs only and answer the question *what* or *whom*

> The captain steers the big **ship**. (steers what? steers the big **ship**)
> The captain calls the **crew**. (calls whom? calls the **crew**)

- An action verb does not always have a direct object.

> The ship sails.     The ship sails across the ocean.

### Linking Verbs

A **linking verb** tells what the subject is or is like. It links the subject with a word or words in the predicate that name or describe the subject. If the word names the subject, it is a **predicate noun**. If it describes the subject, it is a **predicate adjective**.

PREDICATE NOUNS

Anna is a **lifeguard**.

Jennifer is a **runner**.

Who will be the **winner**?

PREDICATE ADJECTIVES

Anna is **cheerful**.

Sue is **strong** and **fast**.

The winner appears **happy**.

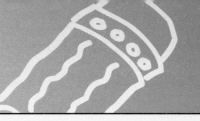

## Linking Verbs (continued)

- A linking verb does not show action.

### Common Linking Verbs

| am | is | are | was | were | will be |
|------|------|-------|-------|------|---------|
| look | feel | taste | smell | seem | appear |

- Some verbs can be either linking verbs or action verbs.

  LINKING: The soup **tastes** salty.

  ACTION: I **taste** the salt in this soup.

## Main Verbs and Helping Verbs

A verb may be one word or a group of words.

The whistle **blew**.                    The runners **have started** the race.

The coach **blew** the whistle.

- A **verb phrase** is made up of a main verb and a helping verb. The **main verb** shows the action. A **helping verb** works with the main verb. The helping verb comes before the main verb.

Kiran **has passed** everyone.        He **has been running** hard.

### Common Helping Verbs

| am | are | were | shall | has |
|----|-----|------|-------|-----|
| is | was | will | have  | had |

## Verb Tense

The **tense** of the verb lets you know *when* something happens.

PRESENT:    Bats **hunt** at night.

PAST:    They **hunted** last night.

FUTURE:    They **will hunt** tonight also.

## Present Tense

A **present tense verb** shows action that is happening now. A present tense verb and its subject must agree in number (singular or plural).

- Add *s* or *es* to most verbs to show the present tense if the subject is singular.

- Do not add *s* or *es* if the subject is plural or is *I* or *you*.

### Rules for Subject-Verb Agreement

| | |
|---|---|
| **Singular subject:** Add *s* or *es* to the verb. | The **driver trains** his dogs. **He teaches** one dog to lead. **He studies** his map. |
| **Plural subject *I* or *you*:** Do not add *s* or *es*. | The **dogs pull** the sleds. **Driver and team travel** far. **They work** together. **I like** your report on dogs. **You write** well. |

## Verb Tense / **Present Tense** (continued)

- Change the spelling of some verbs when adding *s* or *es*.

### Rules for Forming the Present Tense

| | |
|---|---|
| **Most verbs:** <br> Add *s*. | get - get**s** <br> play - play**s** |
| **Verbs ending with *s*, *ch*, *sh*, *x*, and *z*:** <br> Add *es*. | pass - pass**es** <br> punch - punch**es** <br> push - push**es** <br> mix - mix**es** <br> fizz - fizz**es** |
| **Verbs ending with a consonant and *y*:** <br> Change the *y* to *i* and add *es*. | try - tr**ies** <br> empty - empt**ies** |

## Past Tense

A **past tense verb** shows that something already happened. Form the past tense of most verbs by adding *-ed*.

> We **cooked** our dinner over a campfire last night.

- Change the spelling of some verbs when adding *-ed*.

> A squirrel **hoped** for a few crumbs.
>
> It **begged** for a peanut.
>
> Then it **hurried** back to its nest.

(See chart on the next page.)

## Verb Tense / **Past Tense** (continued)

### Rules for Forming the Past Tense

| | |
|---|---|
| **Most verbs:**<br>Add -*ed*. | play - play**ed**<br>reach - reach**ed** |
| **Verbs ending with *e*:**<br>Drop the *e* and add -*ed*. | believ**e** - believ**ed**<br>hop**e** - hop**ed** |
| **Verbs ending with a consonant and *y*:**<br>Change the *y* to *i* and add -*ed*. | stu**dy** - stud**ied**<br>hur**ry** - hurr**ied** |
| **Verbs ending with single vowel and a consonant:**<br>Double the final consonant and add -*ed*. | st**op** - sto**pped**<br>pl**an** - plan**ned** |

## Future Tense

A **future tense verb** tells what is going to happen. Use the main verb with the helping verb *will* or *shall* to form the future tense.

> Nori **will bring** his bird book tomorrow.
>
> Nori and I **will look** for some nests.
>
> **Shall** we **invite** Melissa?

## Verb Tenses with *be* and *have*

*Be* and *have* have special forms in the present and past tense. Change the forms of *be* and *have* to agree with their subjects.

(See chart on the next page.)

## Verb Tenses with *be* and *have* (continued)

| Subject | Form of *be* | | Form of *have* | |
|---|---|---|---|---|
| | **Present** | **Past** | **Present** | **Past** |
| **Singular subjects:** I | am | was | have | had |
| You | are | were | have | had |
| He, she, it (or singular noun) | is | was | has | had |
| **Plural subjects:** We | are | were | have | had |
| You | are | were | have | had |
| They | are | were | have | had |

## Irregular Verbs

**Irregular verbs** have special forms to show the past.

| Irregular Verbs | | |
|---|---|---|
| Verb | Past tense | Past with helping verb |
| bring | brought | (has, have, had) brought |
| come | came | (has, have, had) come |
| go | went | (has, have, had) gone |
| make | made | (has, have, had) made |
| run | ran | (has, have, had) run |
| say | said | (has, have, had) said |
| take | took | (has, have, had) taken |
| think | thought | (has, have, had) thought |
| write | wrote | (has, have, had) written |

## GRAMMAR GUIDE

**Irregular Verbs** (continued)

• Some irregular verbs follow similar patterns.

| Verb | Past Tense | Past with Helping Verb |
|------|-----------|------------------------|
| ring | rang | (has, have, had) rung |
| sing | sang | (has, have, had) sung |
| swim | swam | (has, have, had) swum |
| begin | began | (has, have, had) begun |
| tear | tore | (has, have, had) torn |
| wear | wore | (has, have, had) worn |
| break | broke | (has, have, had) broken |
| speak | spoke | (has, have, had) spoken |
| steal | stole | (has, have, had) stolen |
| choose | chose | (has, have, had) chosen |
| freeze | froze | (has, have, had) frozen |
| blow | blew | (has, have, had) blown |
| grow | grew | (has, have, had) grown |
| know | knew | (has, have, had) known |
| fly | flew | (has, have, had) flown |

## ADJECTIVES

### Definition

An **adjective** is a word that describes a noun or a pronoun.

> **Powerful** lions stared at us.      They seemed **irritated.**

• An adjective tells what kind or how many. It can come before a noun or after a linking verb.

| what kind | **Spotted** fawns were resting. | They looked **peaceful**. |
|-----------|---------------------------------|---------------------------|
| how many | **Three** elephants were eating. | Monkeys did **several** tricks. |

## Adjectives (continued)

- When two or more adjectives are listed together, use a comma to separate them, unless one of the adjectives tells how many.

    **Large, colorful** parrots screeched.     **Two white** geese honked loudly.

## Articles

*A*, *an*, and *the* are special adjectives called **articles**. *A* and *an* refer to any person, place, or thing. *The* refers to a particular person, place, or thing.

    Let's take **a** trip. (any)          It's time for **the** trip. (particular)

| Articles | |
|---|---|
| **a** | Use before singular words that begin with a consonant sound.<br>    **a** jet          **a** high step |
| **an** | Use before singular words that begin with a vowel sound.<br>    **an** engineer     **an** hour |
| **the** | Use before singular and plural words.<br>    **the** answer     **the** plans |

## Demonstrative Adjectives

*This, that, these,* and *those* are demonstrative adjectives. They tell which one.

- *This* and *these* refer to nouns close to the speaker or writer. *That* and *those* refer to nouns farther away.

    **This** book is my favorite.          **That** book is Aja's favorite.

- *This* and *that* are used with singular nouns, *these* and *those* with plural nouns.

    **These** books are mine.          **Those** books are Aja's

## Comparing with Adjectives

To compare two people, places, or things, add -*er* to most adjectives. To compare three or more, add -*est*. Use *more* and *most*, not -*er* and -*est*, with long adjectives.

| | |
|---|---|
| ONE PERSON: | Sy is **tall**. He seems **gigantic.** |
| TWO PERSONS: | Lu is **taller** than Sy. She seems **more gigantic** than he does. |
| THREE OR MORE: | Carlos is **tallest** of all. He seems **most gigantic.** |

• Change the spelling of some adjectives when adding -*er* and -*est*.

### Rules for Comparing with Adjectives

| | |
|---|---|
| 1. **Most adjectives:** Add -*er* or -*est* to the adjective. | bright<br>bright**er**<br>bright**est** |
| 2. **Adjectives ending with *e*:** Drop the *e* and add -*er* or -*est*. | safe<br>saf**er**<br>saf**est** |
| 3. **Adjectives ending with a consonant and *y*:** Change the *y* to *i* and add -*er* or -*est*. | bus**y**<br>bus**ier**<br>bus**iest** |
| 4. **One-syllable adjectives that end with a single vowel and a consonant:** Double the final consonant and add -*er* or -*est*. | flat<br>flat**ter**<br>flat**test** |
| 5. **Some adjectives with two or more syllables:** Use *more* or *most* instead of -*er* or -*est*. | careful<br>**more** careful<br>**most** careful |

## Comparing with Adjectives (continued)

The adjectives *good* and *bad* have special forms for making comparisons.

- Use *better* and *worse* to compare two. Use *best* and *worst* to compare more than two.

ONE: The dress rehearsal of our play was **good**. No one made a **bad** mistake.

TWO: Our first performance was **better**. Our next one was **worse**.

THREE OR MORE: Our last performance was **best**. The third one was **worst**.

| Comparing with *good* and *bad* | | |
|---|---|---|
| Describing one person, place, or thing | good | bad |
| Describing two persons, places, or things | better | worse |
| Describing three or more persons, places, or things | best | worst |

## Proper Adjectives

A proper adjective is formed from a proper noun. A proper adjective begins with a capital letter. When a proper adjective is two words, capitalize both words.

| Proper Noun | Proper Adjective |
|---|---|
| Italy | **Italian** cooking |
| Mexico | **Mexican** rug |
| Switzerland | **Swiss** watch |
| South America | **South American** bird |

# GRAMMAR GUIDE

## ADVERBS

### Definition

An **adverb** is a word that describes a verb and tells *how, when,* or *where.*

HOW: The plane landed **smoothly** at the airport.

WHEN: **Soon** Jeff would see his grandparents at the gate.

WHERE: They were waiting for him **there**.

| How | When | Where |
|---|---|---|
| fast | tomorrow | here |
| hard | later | inside |
| together | again | far |
| happily | often | upstairs |
| quietly | first | downtown |
| secretly | next | somewhere |
| slowly | then | forward |

### Comparing with Adverbs

Use special forms of adverbs to compare actions.

| Rules for Comparing with Adverbs | | |
|---|---|---|
| **Most short adverbs:** Add *-er* or *-est* to the adverb. | late later latest | early earlier earliest |
| **Long adverbs and most adverbs that end with *-ly*:** Use *more* or *most* with the adverb. | often **more** often **most** often | quickly **more** quickly **most** quickly |

## Comparing with Adverbs (continued)

ONE ACTION:    Amy will finish the book **soon**.

She will return the book **promptly.**

TWO ACTIONS:    Amy will finish **sooner** than Jessie will.

She will return the book **more promptly** than Jessie will.

THREE OR MORE:    Amy will finish **soonest** of all.

She will return the book **most promptly** of all.

## PRONOUNS

### Definition

A **pronoun** is a word that takes the place of a noun.

| | |
|---|---|
| Carl watches the swimmers. | **He** watches **them**. |
| The swimmers listen for the whistle. | **They** listen for **it**. |
| Mary held Mary's blue ribbon. | **She** held **her** blue ribbon. |
| Mr. Jones and I clapped loudly. | **We** clapped loudly. |

### Subject Pronouns

There are seven **subject pronouns**. Some are singular, and some are plural.

| Subject Pronouns | |
|---|---|
| **Singular** | **Plural** |
| I | we |
| you | you |
| he, she, it | they |

Bill, will **you** keep time?

Li and Andy, will **you** hand out towels?

Tania and I will record the times. **We** know what to do.

Carlton and Amy will cheer the team. **They** are very loud.

## Subject Pronouns (continued)

- Use **subject pronouns** as subjects of sentences.

    **I** want to compete in a swim meet.     **You** offered some tips.
    **They** have helped improve my speed.

- Use **subject pronouns** after forms of the verb *be*.

    The first swimmer into the water was **I**.

    Did Tina and Angelo win? Yes, the winners were **they**.

- When using *I* with another noun or subject pronoun, always name yourself last.

    **Mel and I** go to every swim meet.   The time keepers at the last one were **Al and I**.

## Object Pronouns

There are seven **object pronouns**.
Some are singular, and some are plural.
(Note that *it* and *you* may be subject or
object pronouns.)

| Object Pronouns | |
|---|---|
| **Singular** | **Plural** |
| me | us |
| you | you |
| him, her, it | them |

Jeremy took <u>Lupe and Carlos</u> on a hike. He took **them** to Crystal Falls.
Dad gave <u>the compass</u> to <u>Rebecca</u>. Dad gave **it** to **her** last night.
Jeremy asked <u>Leroy and me</u> to carry the lunches. He gave **us** a pack.

- Use **object pronouns** after action verbs.

    Dad helped **her** build a campfire.     They built **it** inside a circle of stones.

- Use **object pronouns** after words such as *to, for, about, between,* and *after.*

    Will Jeremy cook dinner for **us**?     Arlyn will do the dishes with **me**.

- When using *me* with another noun or object pronoun, always name yourself last.

    Dad showed **Jeremy and me** how to fish.
    The fish weren't biting for **him and me**.

## Possessive Pronouns

A **possessive pronoun** shows ownership. It replaces a possessive noun.

> Paul's pen is black. He keeps it in **his** pocket.
>
> The blue notebook is Kate's. The pencil is also **hers**.

- There are two kinds of possessive pronouns. Some possessive pronouns appear before nouns. Other possessive pronouns stand alone.

### Two Kinds of Possessive Pronouns

| Possessive pronouns used with nouns | | Possessive pronouns that stand alone | |
|---|---|---|---|
| my | **My** book is green. | mine | The green book is **mine**. |
| your | Clean **your** desk. | yours | **Yours** is messy. |
| his | **His** bike is blue. | his | The red bike is **his**. |
| her | This is **her** house. | hers | **Hers** is the gray house. |
| its | **Its** coat is shaggy. | its | **Its** is the shaggy coat. |
| our | Those are **our** pens. | ours | Those pens are **ours**. |
| your | Take **your** sweaters. | yours | Leave **yours** here. |
| their | **Their** hats are red. | theirs | Those hats are **theirs**. |

## Contractions with Pronouns

You can combine pronouns with the verbs *am, is, are, will, would, have, has,* and *had* to form contractions. A contraction is a shortened form of two words.

- Use an apostrophe (') to replace any letters dropped from the second word.

| Pronoun + Verb | Contraction | Pronoun + Verb | Contraction |
|---|---|---|---|
| I am | I'm | I have | I've |
| he is | he's | he has | he's |
| it is | it's | it has | it's |
| you are | you're | you have | you've |
| they are | they're | they have | they've |
| I will | I'll | I had | I'd |
| you will | you'll | you had | you'd |
| we would | we'd | we had | we'd |

- Do not confuse possessive pronouns with contractions that sound the same. To decide which one to use, think about the meaning of the word.

| Possessive pronouns | Contractions with pronouns |
|---|---|
| your = belonging to you | you're = you are |
| its = belonging to it | it's = it is |

**Your** new dog is really cute.   **You're** very lucky.

**Its** body is long and low.   **It's** a dachshund.

## Double Subjects

Do not use a noun and a pronoun to name the same person, place, or thing.

| INCORRECT | CORRECT |
|---|---|
| <u>Mary</u> <u>she</u> is my sister | **Mary** is my sister. |
| | **She** is my sister. |
| Her <u>hat</u> <u>it</u> is pretty | Her **hat** is pretty. |
| | **It** is pretty. |

## PREPOSITIONS AND PREPOSITIONAL PHRASES

### Definition

A **preposition** relates the noun or the pronoun that follows it to another word in the sentence.

I liked the book <u>with</u> the blue <u>cover</u>.          Sula gave it <u>to</u> <u>me</u>.

### Common Prepositions

| about | before | except | of | through |
|---|---|---|---|---|
| above | behind | for | off | to |
| across | below | from | on | under |
| after | beside | in | out | until |
| along | by | inside | outside | up |
| around | down | into | over | with |
| at | during | near | past | without |

## Prepositional Phrases

A **prepositional phrase** is made up of a preposition, its object, and all the words in between.

> We packed the fruit in our knapsacks.

The **object of the preposition** is the noun or the pronoun that follows the preposition.

> prep.    obj. of prep.                prep. obj. of prep.
>
> I liked the book with the blue **cover**.      Sula gave it to **me**.

- The object of the preposition can be a compound object.

  > We took enough oranges for Manuel and Anita.

- Check the pronoun in a compound object by removing the other object.

  > Jim sat with Ann and **me**. (*Think:* Jim sat with **me**.)
  >
  > E-Ling waved to Alonso and us. (*Think:* E-Ling waved to **us**.)

- A prepositional phrase can be at the beginning, in the middle, or at the end of a sentence.

  > At dawn we began our walk.      The map of the area helped us.
  >
  > The path went by a forest and a large lake.

## ABBREVIATIONS

**Abbreviations** are shortened forms of words. Most abbreviations begin with a capital letter and end with a period. Use abbreviations only in special kinds of writing, such as addresses and lists.

- **Titles**

  Mr. *(Mister)* Mr. Pedro Arupe     Sr. *(Senior)* James Morton, Sr.

  Mrs. *(Mistress)* Mrs. Jane Chang     Jr. *(Junior)* James Morton, Jr.

  Ms. Carla Tower     Dr. *(Doctor)* Dr. Ellen Masters

  **Note:** *Miss* is not an abbreviation and does not end with a period.

- **Words Used in Addresses**

  St. *(Street)*     Blvd. *(Boulevard)*     Pkwy. *(Parkway)*

  Rd. *(Road)*     Rte. *(Route)*     Mt. *(Mount or Mountain)*

  Ave. *(Avenue)*     Apt. *(Apartment)*     Expy. *(Expressway)*

  Dr. *(Drive)*

- **Words Used in Business**

  Co. *(Company)*     Inc. *(Incorporated)*

  Corp. *(Corporation)*     Ltd. *(Limited)*

- **Other Abbreviations**

  Some abbreviations are written in all capital letters, with a letter standing for each important word.

  P.D. *(Police Department)*     P.O. *(Post Office)*

  J.P. *(Justice of the Peace)*     R.N. *(Registered Nurse)*

ABBREVIATIONS (continued)

- **States**

The United States Postal Service uses two capital letters and no period in each of its state abbreviations.

| | | |
|---|---|---|
| AL *(Alabama)* | LA *(Louisiana)* | OH *(Ohio)* |
| AK *(Alaska)* | ME *(Maine)* | OK *(Oklahoma)* |
| AZ *(Arizona)* | MD *(Maryland)* | OR *(Oregon)* |
| AR *(Arkansas)* | MA *(Massachusetts)* | PA *(Pennsylvania)* |
| CA *(California)* | MI *(Michigan)* | RI *(Rhode Island)* |
| CO *(Colorado)* | MN *(Minnesota)* | SC *(South Carolina)* |
| CT *(Connecticut)* | MS *(Mississippi)* | SD *(South Dakota)* |
| DE *(Delaware)* | MO *(Missouri)* | TN *(Tennessee)* |
| FL *(Florida)* | MT *(Montana)* | TX *(Texas)* |
| GA *(Georgia)* | NE *(Nebraska)* | UT *(Utah)* |
| HI *(Hawaii)* | NV *(Nevada)* | VT *(Vermont)* |
| ID *(Idaho)* | NH *(New Hampshire)* | VA *(Virginia)* |
| IL *(Illinois)* | NJ *(New Jersey)* | WA *(Washington)* |
| IN *(Indiana)* | NM *(New Mexico)* | WV *(West Virginia)* |
| IA *(Iowa)* | NY *(New York)* | WI *(Wisconsin)* |
| KS *(Kansas)* | NC *(North Carolina)* | WY *(Wyoming)* |
| KY *(Kentucky)* | ND *(North Dakota)* | |

- **Initials**

Initials are abbreviations that stand for a person's first or middle name. Some names have both a first and a middle initial.

E.B. White *(Elwyn Brooks White)*

T. James Carey *(Thomas James Carey)*

Mr. John M. Gordon *(Mister John Morris Gordon)*

## TITLES

### Underlining

The important words and the first and last words in a title are capitalized. Titles of books, magazines, TV shows, movies, and newspapers are underlined.

<u>The Call of the Wild</u> (book)    <u>Cricket</u> (magazine)    <u>Nova</u> (TV show)
<u>Treasure Island</u> (movie)    <u>The Phoenix Express</u> (newspaper)

Computer Tip: Use italic type for these kinds of titles instead of underlining.

### Quotation Marks with Titles

Titles of short stories, songs, articles, book chapters, and most poems are set off by quotation marks (" ").

"The Necklace" (short story)    "Home on the Range" (song)
"Three Days in the Sahara" (article)    "The Human Brain" (chapter)
"Deer at Dusk" (poem)

## QUOTATIONS

### Quotation Marks with Commas and Periods

Quotation marks are used to set off a speaker's exact words. The first word of a quotation begins with a capital letter. Punctuation belongs *inside* the closing quotation marks. Commas separate a quotation from the rest of the sentence.

"Where," asked the stranger, "is the post office?"
"Please put away your books now," said Mr. Emory.
Linda whispered, "What time is it?"
"It's late," replied Bill. "Let's go!"

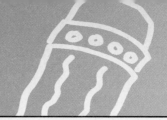

### Writing a Conversation

Begin a new paragraph each time a new person begins speaking.

> "Are you going to drive all the way to Columbus in one day?" asked my Uncle Ben.

> "I really haven't decided," said my father. "I was hoping that you would share the driving with me."

## CAPITALIZATION

1. Capitalize the first word of every sentence.

   <u>W</u>hat a wonderful day this is!

2. Capitalize the pronoun *I*.

   What can <u>I</u> do this afternoon?

3. Capitalize proper nouns. If a proper noun is made up of more than one word, capitalize each important word.

   <u>E</u>mily <u>G</u>. <u>M</u>esse       <u>D</u>istrict of <u>C</u>olumbia       <u>L</u>incoln <u>M</u>emorial

4. Capitalize titles or their abbreviations when used with a person's name.

   <u>G</u>overnor <u>B</u>radford       <u>S</u>enator <u>S</u>mith       <u>D</u>r. <u>L</u>ing

5. Capitalize family titles when they are used as names or as part of names.

   We called <u>A</u>unt Leslie.       May we leave now, <u>G</u>randpa?

6. Capitalize proper adjectives.

   We ate at a <u>F</u>rench restaurant.       That is a <u>N</u>orth <u>A</u>merican custom.
   She is <u>F</u>rench.

7. Capitalize the names of days, months, and holidays.

   The meeting is on the first <u>T</u>uesday in <u>M</u>ay.
   We watched the parade on the <u>F</u>ourth of <u>J</u>uly.

## Capitalization (continued)

**8.** Capitalize the names of groups.

    Aspen Mountain Club        International League

**9.** Capitalize the names of buildings and companies.

    Empire State Building    Able Supply Company    Central School

**10.** Capitalize the first, last, and all important words in a title. Do not capitalize words such as *a, in, and, of,* and *the* unless they begin or end a title.

    Secrets of a Wildlife Watcher    "Growing Up"
    The Los Angeles Times

**11.** Capitalize the first word in the greeting and the closing of a letter.

    Dear Marcia,        Sincerely yours,

**12.** Capitalize the first word of each main topic and subtopic in an outline.

    I. Types of fire departments
      A. Full-time departments
      B. Volunteer departments

## PUNCTUATION

### End Marks

There are three end marks. A *period* (.) ends a declarative or imperative sentence. A *question mark* (?) follows an interrogative sentence. An *exclamation point* (!) follows an exclamatory sentence.

    The notebook is on the shelf. *(declarative)*
    Watch that program at eight tonight. *(imperative)*
    Where does the trail end? *(interrogative)*
    This is your best poem so far! *(exclamatory)*

# GRAMMAR GUIDE

## Apostrophe

To form the possessive of a singular noun, add an apostrophe and *s*.

        doctor's       grandfather's       James's       community's

For a plural noun that ends in *s,* add only an apostrophe.

        sisters'       families'       Boltons'       hound dogs'

For a plural noun that does not end in *s,* add an apostrophe and *s* to form the plural possessive.

        geese's       children's       men's       mice's

Use an apostrophe in contractions in place of dropped letters. Do not use contractions in formal writing.

| | |
|---|---|
| isn't *(is not)* | I'm *(I am)* |
| can't *(cannot)* | they've *(they have)* |
| won't *(will not)* | they'll *(they will)* |
| wasn't *(was not)* | could've *(could have)* |
| we're *(we are)* | would've *(would have)* |
| it's *(it is)* | should've *(should have)* |

## Colon

Use a colon after the greeting in a business letter.

        Dear Mrs. Trimby:                 Dear Realty Homes:

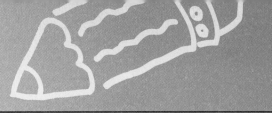
## Comma

A comma (**,**) tells your reader where to pause.

**1.** For words in a series, put a comma after each item except the last. Do not use a comma if only two items are listed.

> We made a salad of lettuce, peppers, and tomatoes.

**2.** Use commas to separate two or more adjectives that are listed together unless one adjective tells how many.

> The fresh, ripe fruit was placed in a bowl.
> One red apple was especially shiny.

**3.** Use a comma before the conjunctions *and, but,* and *or* in a compound sentence.

> Some students were at lunch, but others were studying.

**4.** Use commas after introductory words such as *yes, no, oh,* and *well* when they begin a sentence.

> Yes, it's a perfect day for a picnic. Well, I'll make dessert.

**5.** Use a comma to separate a noun in direct address.

> Gloria, hold this light for me.
> How was the movie, Grandma?
> Can you see, Joe, where I left my glasses?

**6.** Use a comma to separate the month and the day from the year.

> I celebrated my birthday on July 3, 1992.

**7.** Use a comma between the names of a city and a state.

> Denver, Colorado                    Miami, Florida

**8.** Use a comma after the greeting in a friendly letter.

> Dear Tayo,                    Dear Aunt Claudia,

**9.** Use a comma after the closing in a letter.

> Your friend,                    Yours truly,

**Quotation Marks** See Quotations, p. 309.

## PROBLEM WORDS

| Words | Rules | Examples |
|-------|-------|----------|
| can<br><br>may | *Can* means "to be able to do something."<br>*May* means "to be allowed or permitted." | Nellie <u>can</u> read quickly.<br><br><u>May</u> I borrow your book? |
| good<br>well | *Good* is an adjective.<br>*Well* is usually an adverb. It is an adjective only when it refers to health. | The weather looks <u>good</u>.<br>She sings <u>well</u>.<br>Do you feel <u>well</u>? |
| its<br>it's | *Its* is a possessive pronoun.<br>*It's* is a contraction of *it is*. | The dog wagged <u>its</u> tail.<br><u>It's</u> cold today. |
| let<br>leave | *Let* means "to permit or allow."<br>*Leave* means "to go away from" or "to let remain in a place." | Please <u>let</u> me go swimming.<br>I will <u>leave</u> soon.<br><u>Leave</u> it on my desk. |
| sit<br><br>set | *Sit* means "to rest in one place."<br>*Set* means "to place or put." | Please <u>sit</u> in this chair.<br><br><u>Set</u> the vase on the table. |
| teach<br><br>learn | *Teach* means "to give instruction.<br>*Learn* means "to receive instruction. | He <u>teaches</u> us how to dance.<br><br>I <u>learned</u> about history. |
| their<br>there<br><br>they're | *Their* is a possessive pronoun.<br>*There* is an adverb. It may also begin a sentence.<br>*They're* is a contraction of *they are*. | <u>Their</u> coats are on the bed.<br>Is Carlos <u>there</u>?<br><u>There</u> is my book.<br><u>They're</u> going to the store. |
| two<br>to<br>too | *Two* is a number.<br>*To* means "in the direction of."<br>*Too* means "more than enough" and "also." | I bought <u>two</u> shirts.<br>A squirrel ran <u>to</u> the tree.<br>Can we go <u>too</u>? |
| your<br><br>you're | *Your* is a possessive pronoun.<br>*You're* is a contraction for *you are*. | Are these <u>your</u> glasses?<br><br><u>You're</u> late again! |

## ADJECTIVE AND ADVERB USAGE

### Double Comparisons

Never combine *-er* with the word *more*. Do not combine *-est* with the word *most*.

You are a <u>better</u> (not *more better*) artist than I.

The fourth question is the easiest one (not *most easiest*).

### Negatives

A negative is a word that means "no" or "not." Do not use two negatives to express one negative idea.

INCORRECT:  We can't do nothing.

CORRECT:  We <u>can't</u> do <u>anything</u>.

CORRECT:  We <u>can</u> do <u>nothing</u>.

---

**Negative Words**

| | | |
|---|---|---|
| no | no one | never |
| none | nothing | neither |
| nobody | nowhere | |

---

## PRONOUN USAGE

### Agreement

A pronoun must agree with the noun to which it refers.

Kee bought a <u>newspaper</u>. Mary read <u>it</u>.

<u>Jeff and Cindy</u> came to dinner. <u>They</u> enjoyed the meal.

### Double Subjects

Do not use a double subject—a noun and a pronoun—to name the same person, place, or thing.

INCORRECT:  The food it was delicious.

CORRECT:  The food was delicious.

# PROOFREADING CHECKLIST

Check your paper for mistakes. Use the questions below to help you. Correct any mistakes you find. After you have made the corrections, put a check mark in the box next to the question.

- ❑ **1.** Did I indent each paragraph?
- ❑ **2.** Did I make each sentence a complete thought?
- ❑ **3.** Are there any run-on sentences?
- ❑ **4.** Did I spell all words correctly?
- ❑ **5.** Did I use capital letters correctly?
- ❑ **6.** Did I use punctuation marks correctly?
- ❑ **7.** Did I use nouns, verbs, adjectives, and pronouns correctly?

Is there anything else you should look for? Make your own proofreading list on a separate piece of paper.

## PROOFREADING MARKS

| Mark | Explanation | Example |
|------|-------------|---------|
| ¶ | Begin a new paragraph. Indent the paragraph. | ¶ We went to an air show last Saturday. Eight jets flew across the sky in the shape of *V*'s, *X*'s, and diamonds. |
| ∧ | Add letters, words, or sentences. | The leaves were red ∧*and* orange. |
| ℘ | Take out words, sentences, and punctuation marks. Correct spelling. | The sky is bright *blue* blew. Huge clouds move quickly. |
| / | Change a capital letter to a small letter. | The F̸ireflies blinked in the dark. |
| ☰ | Change a small letter to a capital letter. | New York city is exciting. |